Gamification

PRACTICAL GUIDES FOR LIBRARIANS

About the Series

This innovative series written and edited for librarians by librarians provides authoritative, practical information and guidance on a wide spectrum of library processes and operations. Books in the series are focused, describing practical and innovative solutions to a problem facing today's librarian and delivering step-by-step guidance for planning, creating, implementing, managing, and evaluating a wide range of services and programs.

The books are aimed at beginning and intermediate librarians needing basic instruction/guidance in a specific subject and at experienced librarians who need to gain knowledge in a new area or guidance in implementing a new program/service.

About the Series Editor

The **Practical Guides for Librarians** series was conceived by and is edited by M. Sandra Wood, MLS, MBA, AHIP, FMLA, Librarian Emerita, Penn State University Libraries. M. Sandra Wood was a librarian at the George T. Harrell Library, the Milton S. Hershey Medical Center, College of Medicine, Pennsylvania State University, Hershey, PA, for over thirty-five years, specializing in reference, educational, and database services. Ms. Wood worked for several years as a development editor for Neal-Schuman Publishers.

Ms. Wood received an MLS from Indiana University and an MBA from the University of Maryland. She is a fellow of the Medical Library Association and served as a member of MLA's Board of Directors from 1991 to 1995. Ms. Wood is founding and current editor of *Medical Reference Services Quarterly*, now in its thirty-fifth volume. She also was founding editor of the *Journal of Consumer Health on the Internet* and the *Journal of Electronic Resources in Medical Libraries* and served as editor/coeditor of both journals through 2011.

Titles in the Series

Gamification
A Practical Guide
for Librarians

Elizabeth McMunn-Tetangco

PRACTICAL GUIDES FOR LIBRARIANS, NO. 31

ROWMAN & LITTLEFIELD
Lanham • Boulder • New York • London

Published by Rowman & Littlefield
A wholly owned subsidiary of The Rowman & Littlefield Publishing Group, Inc.
4501 Forbes Boulevard, Suite 200, Lanham, Maryland 20706
www.rowman.com

Unit A, Whitacre Mews, 26-34 Stannary Street, London SE11 4AB

British Library Cataloguing in Publication Information Available

Library of Congress Cataloging-in-Publication Data Available

ISBN 978-1-4422-7913-1 (pbk : alk. paper)
ISBN 978-1-4422-7914-8 (electronic)

∞™ The paper used in this publication meets the minimum requirements of American
National Standard for Information Sciences—Permanence of Paper for Printed Library
Materials, ANSI/NISO Z39.48-1992.

Printed in the United States of America

Contents

Illustrations

Preface

Gamification, or the application of game attributes to non-game settings, has gained momentum in many fields in recent years, and it's easy to see why. After all, anyone who has lost track of time in the middle of a board game or soccer match can testify that games can be highly engaging. Games in libraries are not a new concept—many libraries provide board and video game collections, and library instruction sessions often include games such as modified versions of Jeopardy! or scavenger hunts designed to teach students about library services.

Gamification takes this promise of engagement one step further to deploy games as tools. The hope is that if something is fun, people will want to do it. This exchange of work for enjoyment, however, opens some gamification initiatives to suggestions of manipulation. Are you returning books on time because you are a responsible library patron, for instance? Or are you just doing it because you want to win points? Worse still, there is an abundance of evidence to show that people's interest in activities plummets when added rewards are removed—even if those same people had previously been participating in the activities for sheer enjoyment. Games and gamification efforts skate on the blade of these issues, and in planning them, you need to consider why games are a good venue for accomplishing what you want for your library and your patrons.

Because the world of games is so vast, this book does not focus exclusively on gamification in libraries. Instead, we will look at the use of games in libraries more generally—both games played for their own sake and games used in order to increase patron motivation and interest. Many aspects of games are considered here, from the trend of personalization in both games and other library services, the application of types of games to different library scenarios, and game design in general to how to best work with library and community partners and how to assess games at their completion. Particular attention is paid to the importance of considering your patrons and community as you work on game projects—what works beautifully in one setting may encounter snags and difficulties in another. Whenever possible, real-life games that have been used in libraries are presented as examples.

Each chapter includes details and ideas from the Library Stars Tour game, a fictional scavenger hunt–style activity developed to illustrate many of the concepts in this book. Though the Library Stars Tour game is set in the context of library orientation for new students at a small college, it certainly does not apply only to this setting, and pieces of it may well be applicable to public libraries, school libraries, and other areas.

Gamification: A Practical Guide for Librarians is divided into ten chapters that collectively explore some of the issues and choices you will face as you begin to design games and game-inspired projects. Because there are so many different types of games, some of these chapters may be more or less relevant to your particular project—you are encouraged to skip between chapters and use them as needed while you work on your game.

In chapter 1, "Why Games?" you will learn about the potential appeal of games and how they can be effective as learning tools. The distinction between games and gamification is explored here as well as some potential drawbacks you may face in using games for learning. This is a good place to start if you are asking yourself why you might want to use games in the first place. In addition, this chapter introduces the Library Stars Tour game, which will be discussed further in subsequent chapters as an example.

Chapter 2, "Personalization," discusses the use of individualized services and offerings tailored toward specific people. Amazon book suggestions are an example of personalization, for instance, and there are ways personalization can be used in game settings as well. While personalization can involve choice, it can also potentially limit your patrons' access to materials.

Chapter 3, "Setting Goals and Objectives," focuses on how you will set goals and objectives for your game or project. Goals will help you in a number of ways, including giving you a framework to use when determining whether your project was a success and providing structure you can use in game design.

Chapter 4, "Designing Your Project," delves into game design, which could be a book in and of itself! Game design is an art, and different games will require different ways of thinking. This chapter will encourage you to think about your audience and their needs, interests, and desires as you plan your game.

Chapter 5, "Identifying Partners and Making a Case," discusses identifying potential partners for your project and how you might argue to stakeholders and other interested parties for its importance. Included here are tips for identifying possible partners and working effectively in groups. Successful collaborations between librarians and other community members often provide rich results.

Chapter 6, "Types of Games," provides a survey of different types of games and will help you determine which type of game may be the best fit for your project. Of particular note in this chapter are role-playing games, video games, board games, scavenger hunts, and digital badges.

Chapter 7, "Using Games in Instruction," is an overview of games used during library instruction, which can be a particularly fruitful venue. Discussed in this chapter are the use of flipped instruction to make room for games; how to align games with instruction goals; and how other librarians have used games as learning tools.

Chapter 8, "Game Accessibility," explores ways you can make your game accessible to as many patrons as possible. Accessible games will benefit a larger number of people than those that make assumptions about their players, and this can help you reach patrons who might otherwise not hear as much about your services.

Chapter 9, "Game Assessment," provides strategies you can use to assess your game and—more importantly—use your results to improve patron experiences in the future. Potential assessment questions are listed in this chapter in addition to thoughts on the strengths and relevance of various assessment formats.

Chapter 10, "Themes and Predictions," discusses ways that games and real life overlap and identifies some themes that you may want to consider as you design your game. Also included are thoughts about the future of games and how they might be used in libraries from here on out.

The library world is full of all types of inspiring and enjoyable games, and librarians and library staff are a highly creative and innovative group. Whether you approach this book in hopes of finding inspiration or as a way to find step-by-step guidance as you begin to develop your own game, I sincerely encourage you to take in the breadth of the opportunities around you and to allow yourself to find motivation and insight from your patrons, community, and colleagues as you design games of your own.

Acknowledgments

Thank you to my colleagues at UC Merced for being a continual source of inspiration and support. In addition, thanks are due to Rowman & Littlefield, and in particular to Sandy Wood, who made the process of writing this book much smoother than it might have been otherwise. Lastly, thank you to Keith and James.

Why Games?

GAMES CAN GIVE US better worlds. The rules can change, life can be fair, and the gravest of mistakes can be repealed. Everything happens for a reason.

Framed this way, it is easy to understand why games have such an enduring hold on the people who play them: they allow us to live different lives and become different—perhaps more exciting—people. Games can captivate their players, causing them to lose track of time as they immerse themselves fully in new worlds—think of video game players who forget their surroundings or children who ask to play just one more round of a board game before going to bed. More than that, games can help their players learn.

Game rules are different than the rules of life, and every new game requires its players to learn a specific rule system. Tetris players need to understand how shapes fit together. Super Mario Brothers players need to accept that squashing mushrooms will help them earn points. Uno players need to make quick connections between numbers and colors to rapidly get rid of cards. Many games build in levels and strategies that help players learn as they move forward—think of video-game levels that increase in difficulty as players work to get the hang of them or quiz shows that start off with easy questions and then become more complicated.

Because of the wide appeal of games, they hold a lot of potential for use in libraries. Games can be created for outreach, instruction, access to services, and social media. They can help librarians forge stronger connections with their patrons and can establish the library as a welcoming, friendly space. Games can be large or small, engrossing or casual, and they can be tailored to fit the context, needs, and spaces of any sort of library.

"The designers of many good games have hit on profoundly good methods of getting people to learn and to enjoy learning," writes James Paul Gee, "furthermore, it turns out that these methods are similar in many respects to cutting-edge principles being discovered in research on human learning" (2010, 15). Video game designers need to care about learning because if potential players can't learn their games, they won't buy them. Games help players learn, according to Gee, by doing several things: empowering players and making them part of the action; customizing the game to meet player preferences and needs; allowing players to assume an identity that they care about; and giving players control at a distance in order to more fully immerse them in the world of the game (2010).

Mary J. Snyder Broussard, the designer of quite a few library game experiences, writes, "While we talk about designing *games*, we are actually designing *experiences* for the players. . . . To create a good experience for the players, we need to be in touch with what they want" (2014, 208). Dovetailing patron expectations, desire for new experiences, and library goals with games can result in more engaging, interesting, and productive library activities.

Games, Game-Based Learning, and Gamification

There has been some effort to differentiate between *games*, which is defined here as activities engaged in by players voluntarily for fun; *game-based learning*, which establishes specific learning outcomes as the goals of a game activity; and *gamification*, in which elements of games such as points or badges are bestowed upon people who complete various aspects of an otherwise non–game-related activity. Friday family board-game nights fall squarely into the games category. Steven Isaacs cites games like The Oregon Trail, where players learn about the experiences of settlers and decision making as an example of game-based learning (Isaacs 2015). Charts with family member names and as-yet-to-be completed chores family members can finish and then be rewarded for by stickers and other treats fall into gamification. Gamification provides rewards to players who succeed in the goals of activities, and a major focus is on completion rather than on intrinsic motivation. In a library context, a game might include video game nights that encourage college students to visit the library and socialize with other students and librarians, while gamification might offer incentives and a leaderboard to celebrate patrons who make wide use of library materials. Isaacs discusses a stock-market game he played in high school as an example of game-based learning: after learning about the stock market through the game in class, he (along with several family members) invested real money and made a profit (Isaacs 2015).

A key difference between games, game-based learning, and gamification concerns the motivational reasons why people play. Games generally are played by people who want to play them just because, whereas gamification entices cooperation or participation through external motivation. Game and gamification examples are shown in table 1.1.

Table 1.1. Games vs. Gamification Examples

GAME EXAMPLES	GAMIFICATION EXAMPLES
Trivia nights	Giving students points for returning materials on time
Library scavenger hunts (completed independently of classes)	Using a class leaderboard to track how many pages each student has read
Book-theme parties and activities	Jeopardy!-style review after instruction

Depending on how gamification is structured, it runs the risk of being perceived as manipulative. While some patrons will appreciate being able to track their progress and reap rewards for doing their research (think of the popularity of step trackers and apps that record athletic activity), other patrons may not be as interested and may not want to take part. Whenever possible, gamification efforts should be voluntary for your patrons, and the incentives received should not be so great that they become the sole purpose of the activity, thus turning the game simply into a mechanism for getting rewards.

It is also perhaps worth noting that, in this book, there is not a great distinction made between library gamification efforts and library games. The focus, rather, is on how you might use games and game principles at your library in order to more fully connect with patrons. Some examples highlighted in these pages will bear hallmarks of gamification, and others won't. Still others will not fit neatly into either category. However, all of them illustrate ways in which games can be used in library settings and may serve as inspiration as you think about ways to spice up services in your own context.

⑥ Creating Flow Experiences

In *Flow: The Psychology of Optimal Experience*, psychologist Mihaly Csikszentmihalyi defines optimal experiences as times when "instead of being buffeted by anonymous forces, we do feel in control of our actions, masters of our own fate" (1990, 3). These experiences, according to Csikszentmihalyi, can allow players to enter into what he calls *flow*, which is, as he describes it, "the state in which people are so involved in an activity that nothing else seems to matter; the experience itself is so enjoyable that people will do it, even at great cost, for the sheer sake of doing it" (1990, 4).

Games can be especially conducive to promoting these feelings in their players because games exist outside everyday life, and because they include rules and structures that allow participants to feel like their actions are meaningful. Games do not have to be life changing to have this impact—they just have to allow their players to have a good time and feel a sense of control over their lives. While not all games allow players to enter into these states, the fact that so many do helps to explain game popularity and why people will often choose to play games rather than participate in other activities.

You might also think of this as a focus on keeping your activity fun—educational games often get a bad reputation for being boring or rote, and for many of them this is not undeserved. Since games (and many game-based projects) rely on the voluntary participation of players, the sense of enjoyment and accomplishment that games provide cannot be overstated. Libraries may have an advantage in this field, as generally patrons visit library buildings and use library services because they want to, not because they have to. Still, it's important to make sure that library activities and game-inspired events are worth their time.

Csikszentmihalyi identifies eight elements of enjoyment that may be present during an activity. Not all of them need to be present at the same time for a participant to report having enjoyed something, although he notes they often are.

First, the experience usually occurs when we confront tasks we have the capability of completing. Second, we must be able to concentrate on what we are doing. Third and fourth, the concentration is usually possible because the task includes clear goals and feedback. Fifth, one acts with a deep but effortless involvement that removes from awareness the worries and frustrations of everyday life. Sixth, enjoyable experiences allow people to exercise a sense of control over their actions. Seventh, concern for the self disappears, yet paradoxically the sense of self emerges stronger after the flow experience is over. Finally, the sense of duration of time is altered; hours pass by in minutes, and minutes can stretch out to seem like hours. (1990, 49)

Since your activity will rely on players choosing to take part, creating an activity that is inherently appealing to them is important. Csikszentmihalyi's elements can be applied to a wide variety of activities, but the idea of fun must not be added as an afterthought. After all, there are few things less fun than enforced cheer.

Appeal to Various Age Groups

Although much of the literature about games and gamification focuses on video games and their use with younger patrons, games of all kinds can appeal to patrons of all ages. A study conducted by Steve Hoppes, Carole Hally, and Lee Sewell found that older adults were also very interested in games. This particular study, whose participants lived in assisted living, adult daycare, or nursing home situations, in addition to some who lived independently, identified dominoes, checkers, and bingo as being of special interest to subjects (2000). While many gamification efforts involve using game elements to make existing services more fun, it may also be valuable to think about ways events like game and theme nights and informal competitions might fit into your library's schedule.

Nor should there be an assumption that older patrons will only want to play board games or bingo—depending on the interest level in a particular community, you may have success with activities that appeal to all ages. Patrons from many different backgrounds and generations may enjoy the opportunity to interact as a large community. It may be easy to forget that people of all ages can enjoy each other's company and insight.

Increasing Interest in Games

Games and gamification are aspects of a trend that libraries have been circling for several years now, for a few reasons. Chief among these reasons are that (1) games are popular and have a good track record for appealing to lots of different patrons; and (2) technology innovations have now made it much easier for people to connect with games wherever they are, at any time. In addition, the growing ubiquity of social media platforms has allowed games—which may have once taken place mainly where people gathered together—to take on a more central role at any time. People can now play games while waiting in the grocery store checkout line, riding public transportation, or sitting by themselves at home. The Entertainment Software Association (ESA) released a report in 2015 that says that over 155 million Americans are video game users, and that of those, 42 percent play video games for at least three hours every week. Players' favorite games overall are social games, action games, and puzzle/board/card or game-show games. The ESA's 2016 report notes that games appeal to a variety of people, with women—counter to many stereotypes—making up 41 percent of game purchasers. In 2016 the average age of a game player was thirty-five, and the average age of a female player was 44. This growing popularity, combined with ease of access, may mean that there will be more people playing games more frequently in all kinds of contexts fairly soon. The "NMC Horizon

Report: 2013 Higher Education Edition" takes note of this in its section on games and gamification, pointing out that

> anyone who owns a smartphone or tablet can become a gamer. Free mobile games abound, and the most popular have become widely used outlets for social interaction and connecting family and friends, such as "Words with Friends"—a modern take on Scrabble. Social networking features of a mobile game support the prevalence of game play in a culture that is increasingly concerned with staying in touch and being connected all of the time; in this sense, the appeal of online games is not just about who is playing, but who in one's personal network is playing—and winning. (New Media Consortium 2013, 20)

The NMC report anticipates that the time-to-adoption horizon, or how long it will take for gamification and game-based learning to be widely in use, is two to three years.

Psychological Impact of Games

Playing is one of the ways children begin to make sense of and understand the world. Play can take the form of creating new worlds and situations or of simulating the small dramas of everyday life. Children might take inspiration from watching their families cook, for example, or from watching sports games. They might address issues in their play worlds that assist them in processing their emotions and experiences. They can also create lush fantasy worlds to house the ideas and characters that interest them.

The Portland Children's Museum in Portland, Oregon, makes use of many of children's desires to act out the adult lives they see around them by including permanent exhibits that allow children to shop in a mini grocery store complete with cash registers, play food, and shopping carts; or to work in a pet hospital where they can weigh stuffed animals, use a stethoscope, and learn more about how to care for their pets. Both of these exhibits, along with others, allow children to play by pretending to be adults in the world they see around them—adults who might have jobs, families to feed, and animal companions that need medical attention. The popularity of these exhibits and others like them testifies to the importance of allowing children to learn by playing in a setting where they can experiment and grow, often trying on new identities and situations.

Although there is less information about the effect of play on adults, it is clear that games can have an impact on people even after childhood. Adult social media users, for instance, flock to play games like Candy Crush Saga, a puzzle game featuring various candies, and FarmVille, which allows users to interact with others while they simulate running a farm. In 2013, one out of every twenty-three Facebook users played Candy Crush Saga, and the game had been installed over 500 million times on various platforms (Webster 2013). Fantasy football leagues represent another kind of gameplay that appeals to adults, with participants staying up-to-date on trends and players in an attempt to assemble the most successful team possible. In 2012, the video game industry was worth an estimated $67 billion dollars and was predicted to grow even larger, surpassing the revenues made by both the film and music industries (Morford et al. 2014). Outside of games that rely on technology, any quick weekend visit to a local park on a sunny afternoon will most likely afford views of adults playing basketball, soccer, Frisbee, and more.

In the last few years, researchers have begun to explore how a general affinity for games and game-like activity might be harnessed to have a positive impact on players and participants. For example, in a 2010 study carried out by Andrea Grimes, Vasudhara

Kantroo, and Rebecca E. Grinter, OrderUP, a game for mobile phones that focused on helping adults make healthy food choices, was able to encourage five players out of an initial group of twelve to dramatically change their thoughts about food. OrderUP's premise is that the player is a restaurant server who must take customer health into consideration as they make recommendations about possible meals. Each interaction includes information about the customer and three different meal options, which vary in terms of their health impact. The researchers were able to see that people went from not paying attention to whether the foods they ate were healthy to using potential health impact as one of their primary areas of focus. Additionally, eight of the participants in the study reported that using OrderUP encouraged them to change their eating habits (Grimes, Kantroo, and Grinter 2010). The researchers attributed this success partly to the mobile game format, which allowed players to log on any time they had a free moment, and to the game's focus on character avatars and food selection because these appealed to their specific audience. Since the players could choose to log on at any time as long as they played at least once a week, they retained a high level of autonomy, which may also have contributed to the game's appeal (2010).

Games have contributed to efforts at combating other perceived personal and societal issues as well. Multiple games have been developed to improve participant fitness, encourage sustainable environmental practices, and teach students more effectively at various levels (Morford et al. 2014).

SuperBetter, a game described in a book of the same name by Jane McGonigal, for example, purports to help players manage any number of potential issues, including anxiety, chronic pain, and lack of confidence. Effectively, McGonigal's strategy allows a participant to approach hardships in real life as if they are issues that can be surmounted by using game-completion techniques: try again; learn from mistakes; set achievable, small goals that slowly build. McGonigal draws on research that shows the clear benefits of game play in specific situations, including medical procedures. For example, Snow World, designed by researchers at the University of Washington, is a virtual reality video game in which players wear a headset and explore a fictional, frozen landscape with a joystick. The game has been tested in clinical trials focused on treatment of burn victims. According to McGonigal, "This VR [virtual reality] game reduced pain by a whopping *30 to 50 percent*. For the most severe burn patients, the game proved to have a bigger impact on their pain and overall suffering than the morphine they also received" (2015, 30). Effectively, immersion in the game environment of Snow World allowed patients to avoid feeling pain from invasive medical procedures and granted them a reprieve they might not have been able to find elsewhere, results that hint at the power games hold to make hard situations better. While games and game elements in library situations most likely will not have these sorts of life-changing ramifications, acknowledging the power of games is a useful step in planning your activity.

Games provide a venue for organizations ranging from libraries to schools to businesses to engage more fully with their users by connecting with them on a deep psychological level and providing them with ways to explore spaces and services more fully. Games and game elements seem to appeal to human desires on a very baseline level. Morford et al. acknowledge this: "Successful game design appears to align well with principles and concepts within behavior analysis. That humans collectively play over three billion hours of video games per week is strong evidence of this" (2014, 37). In short, people are interested in games and are willing to spend time on them, and games can be used to effect positive change on their players. Developing games that appeal to patron needs and interests can help libraries connect more fully with the people who matter to them.

⊚ Possible Drawbacks to Game Elements in a Library Setting

Although it is clear that using elements of games and gamification can have a wide array of benefits in a library setting, there are also potentially some drawbacks to using game elements that should be considered.

One possible drawback is that game elements, used in a library setting, are probably not going to have all of the inherent, built-in appeal of a game that a patron has decided to play on his or her own. Because games in a library by necessity may need to connect to a goal or outcome the library is hoping to attain, they are not generally engineered just to be fun or to tell an engaging story, and this may have an impact on their success. Player motivation is a crucial consideration as you think about whether and how to develop game-related activities at your library, and it is therefore important to note that people are much more likely to stick with something if they are intrinsically motivated to do so. There is much evidence that providing rewards for activities that participants have previously engaged in out of inherent interest decreases those same patrons' later motivation to continue with the activities (Deci, Koestner, and Ryan 1999).

Many game designers differentiate between what they call *edutainment*—or educationally driven projects that incorporate some aspect of entertainment in order to be more engaging to users—and *serious games*, which exist solely to engage their players in the world of a game. Because of the diverging purposes of these differing types of games, what will work in one context will not necessarily work in another. Dennis Charsky puts this as follows:

> Teaching lower order thinking skills, facts, concepts, and procedures are essential to fields of study, but typically that is all edutainment attempts to teach. Edutainment typically makes little or no attempt at trying to teach gamers how to apply their knowledge, analyze their understanding, synthesize their perceptions, or evaluate their learning. (2010, 180)

Whereas much educational gaming focuses on quickly learning concrete skills, part of the appeal of more serious games is a player's ability to move beyond skill attainment and instead participate more fully in an established and developed game world. This can involve developing relationships with other players and characters, earning points for accomplishing various tasks, or setting goals outside simple game play. For example, Charsky describes a game called Virtual Leader, where players can determine what success will look like in their particular context. "The competition in Virtual Leader, and many other commercial and serious games," writes Charsky, "does not solely exist with achieving victory but is coupled with negotiating difficult situations, analyzing the feedback [players] receive, and applying this analysis to new, yet similar, situations" (2010, 182). Charsky notes that players of serious games don't always just want to win—they can be motivated instead to become part of the game and participate more fully in its environs and storyline.

Of additional importance is the question of tone. The tone of your activity is something that may be of special concern, which leads to another potential drawback. If, for instance, you develop a game or activity that appears to minimize library services or events, your patrons could interpret this as a message that they do not need to care about them, even if this was not your intention. To use an example of this, though one not directly related to libraries, in late 2015, Airbnb—a service that works to connect people visiting an area with residents who are interested in renting out their homes on a short-term basis—ran several ads in San Francisco that attempted to lightheartedly make suggestions for how the city could use the tax dollars Airbnb had paid. For example, "Dear Public Library System, We hope you use some of the $12 million in hotel taxes to keep the library open later. Love, Airbnb" (Swan 2015). Although the ads were probably designed to highlight the ways Airbnb added to the local economy, they did not come across as intended, and Airbnb ended up issuing a public apology after the ads were widely criticized on social media. The ads came down right away. This is a lesson to keep in mind for anyone designing a project for public release, and it may be good to think about as you consider how to publicize and carry out your project.

The design of and reaction to your activity will largely depend on patron demographics, the tone of previous library communications and services, and an understanding of your overall community. However, it may be useful to think about your goals and how your project will help you to meet them in the specific context of your library.

The Library Stars Tour Game

As you progress through this book, the Library Stars Tour game, which has been created as an example, will serve to illustrate many of the suggestions and ideas presented here. Though the game doesn't exist outside this book, its concept is similar to many tour or scavenger hunt–style projects conducted in real life by various libraries. The game's overall aim is to show how the ideas presented here might take shape in an actual library activity that is similar in scope and content to many games already in use.

Setting

The Library Stars Tour game is set in an academic library with a medium-size student population where most students take an introductory writing class during their first or second semester. The university is situated in an area that has been noted for its beauty and proximity to several movie studios; because of this, many celebrities have homes close by, and there is a thriving celebrity-homes tour market. Thus, the Stars Tour game is positioned as a nod to the university environment and reflects the community setting of the campus. The celebrity-related theme also allows some easy connections to local businesses, such as movie theaters and off-campus stores. This allows students to become more familiar with area recreational opportunities, and it helps connect the campus with the town it calls home.

In addition to this local slant, the Stars Tour theme is designed to be slightly silly. It is hoped that this will reduce library anxiety among first-year students and encourage them to have a good time and to return to the library in the future.

Academic Context

Students are assigned to take the tour by their writing instructors, and they can choose to take it any time the library is open. The tour further reflects the situation of the campus because introductory writing classes focus on writing as a craft rather than research, and as such they do not include a library instruction session. The tour anticipates that students will need to conduct research in subsequent semesters and is designed in part to remind students about library resources.

Tour Basics

During the tour, students travel in groups or alone through the library, answering questions, meeting library staff and student workers, and learning about how the library can help them be successful. Upon arrival at the library, they receive a packet of tour information. They can choose the format of this information, which can be provided as a paper version; as a website they can access via a QR code that can be scanned into their phone; or as a program installed on a device that they can check out at the library circulation desk. Materials in the packet include

- Tour instructions
- Library maps
- A photo of a book with a fame/celebrity theme
- A photo of the entrance to a library reading room
- A photo of a movie database
- Three raffle tickets per team member
- An autograph booklet
- An answer sheet for questions

Over the course of the tour, students progress through the library, answering questions and collecting autographs from staff members as needed. Questions are designed to give students a physical survey of the library and to encourage them to interact with library staff. Questions and instructions include

1. Where you go in the library depends on what you need! Find the Circulation Desk, and ask a friendly staff member to sign your autograph book.
2. Need to screen a movie? The Media Viewing Room has you covered! What floor can you find it on?
3. Look at the photo of the book included with your materials. Library call numbers will help you determine where it's located. Use the library maps to find the book and write down the code you find on its spine.
4. Need to find a database? Go to the computer labs on the fifth floor and open the library's webpage. Once you're there, click on the Databases link. Bonus points if you're able to get the computer lab student assistant to sign your autograph book!
5. Now that you're looking at databases, enter the name of the database in the photo you received in your packet into the Database search bar. What types of information can you find here?
6. Sometimes even stars like to curl up with a good book. Find the library Reading Room and take a look around. What do you think you might read here?

The tour ends at the circulation desk, where library staff check answers, distribute raffle tickets, and record tour-participant names and e-mail addresses, which can then be reported to assigning faculty. At the end of the semester, a raffle will be held, and students who completed the tour will be eligible to win gift baskets and prizes, including movie tickets, microwave popcorn, sunglasses, and library pens, stickers, and other small giveaway items.

Overall, the tour's goal is to familiarize students with library staff, spaces, and services and help them feel comfortable asking for help and spending time in the library.

Possible Platforms

Though tours in this format can include paper instructions, there are also a good number of software companies that provide platforms for tours and games, some of which include additional multimedia options. One benefit to using a software platform rather than a paper version of tour instructions is that many platforms can save answers and help you process them. Some of these platforms are listed below, though this list is not comprehensive.

Articulate Storyline: www.articulate.com/products/storyline-why.php

Edventure Builder: www.edventurebuilder.com/

GooseChase: www.goosechase.com/

Kahoot! https://getkahoot.com/

Twine: https://twinery.org/

QR codes: These can be created for free at many sites online.

Key Points

This chapter has discussed reasons why games can be effective learning tools, and it has emphasized points to keep in mind when planning to implement games as educational objects. Focusing on player enjoyment, choice, and context when you begin to implement game services and activities can help you make your patrons' game experiences as rewarding as possible.

- Good game design emphasizes patron learning.
- Games can be useful tools outside of a traditional, educationally focused environment.
- While games are generally voluntary sources of entertainment, gamification adds game elements to the outside world.
- Games that reward people for doing things they are already interested in doing can eventually decrease those same peoples' interest.
- Games appeal to people of all age groups, not just to children and young adults.
- Awareness of who your patrons are and what they need and want from the library will help you design your game.
- Good games are successful in part because people want to play them.

In the next chapter, you will learn about how providing personalized patron experiences can both enhance and in some cases detract from the goals of your game.

References

Charsky, Dennis. 2010. "From Edutainment to Serious Games: A Change in the Use of Game Characteristics." *Games and Culture* 5, no. 2 (February): 177–98.

Csikszentmihalyi, Mihaly. 1990. *Flow: The Psychology of Optimal Experience*. New York: Harper & Row.

Deci, Edward L., Richard Koestner, and Richard M. Ryan. 1999. "A Meta-Analytic Review of Experiments Examining the Effects of Extrinsic Rewards on Intrinsic Motivation." *Psychological Bulletin* 125 (6): 627–68.

Entertainment Software Association. 2015 and 2016. "Essential Facts about the Computer and Video Game Industry." www.theesa.com/wp-content/uploads/2015/04/ESA-Essential-Facts-2015.pdf and www.theesa.com/wp-content/uploads/2016/04/ESA-Essential-Facts-2016.pdf.

Gee, James Paul. 2010. "Learning by Design: Games as Learning Machines." *Interactive Educational Multimedia* 8:15–23.

Grimes, Andrea, Vasudhara Kantroo, and Rebecca E. Grinter. 2010. "Let's Play! Mobile Health Games for Adults." *Proceedings of the 12th ACM International Conference on Ubiquitous Computing*. Copenhagen, Denmark (September 26–29, 2010): 241–50.

Hoppes, Steve, Carole Hally, and Lee Sewell. 2000. "An Interest Inventory of Games for Older Adults." *Physical & Occupational Therapy in Geriatrics* 18 (2): 71–83.

Isaacs, Steven. 2015. "The Difference between Gamification and Game-Based Learning." *ACSD InService.* http://inservice.ascd.org/the-difference-between-gamification-and-game-based-learning/.

McGonigal, Jane. 2015. *Superbetter: A Revolutionary Approach to Getting Stronger, Happier, Braver, and More Resilient.* New York: Penguin Press.

Morford, Zachary H. et al. 2014. "Gamification: The Intersection between Behavior Analysis and Game Design Technologies." *Behavior Analyst* 37 (1): 25–40.

New Media Consortium. 2013. "NMC Horizon Report: 2013 Higher Education Edition." http://redarchive.nmc.org/publications/2013-horizon-report-higher-ed.

Snyder Broussard, Mary J. 2014. "Knowing When to Create a Library Game." In *Games in Libraries*, edited by Breanne A. Kirsch, 30–42. Jefferson, NC: McFarland & Company.

Swan, Rachel. 2015. "Airbnb Apologizes for Much-Criticized Ads on S.F. Bus Shelters." *SFGate.* www.sfgate.com/bayarea/article/Airbnb-apologizes-for-much-criticized-ads-on-S-F-6585674.php.

Webster, Andrew. 2013. "Half a Billion People Have Installed 'Candy Crush Saga.'" *The Verge.* www.theverge.com/2013/11/15/5107794/candy-crush-saga-500-million-downloads.

CHAPTER 2

Personalization

> IN THIS CHAPTER

▷ What personalization is

▷ Examples of ways librarians and others are already using personalization techniques, such as digital badges, to provide more customized experiences for their users

▷ Some disadvantages and dangers to using personalization as you plan activities for your library

FROM SODA CANS inscribed with our names to filter bubbles that show us just the news a search engine thinks we're interested in, personalization seems to be everywhere, and as such it has definite implications for gamification efforts. People working in education, business, and other fields have recognized personalization's potential and have worked to develop services tailored specifically toward individuals in an attempt to better reach them. Although marketing efforts and library outreach and instruction are different beasts, there may be some overlap in terms of their existential need to connect with users. This chapter will explore what personalization is, its benefits and drawbacks in a library setting, and what you may want to keep in mind as you decide whether or not to incorporate it into your services.

Personalization: An Overview

Personalization is, simply, the adaptation of services and offerings to individuals. Think of the convenience of book suggestions at the bottom of an Amazon search. While this list may not end up completely guiding your reading, it can help you find new authors based on what you already know you like. Conversely, however, it may also indirectly limit your reading by encouraging you to focus on titles similar to those you have already read. In the library context, personalization might mesh with gamification to produce events and activities tailored toward the goals and needs of individual participants, but care must be taken to ensure that privacy is not violated and that users are not inadvertently presented with only one point of view.

Reasons for Personalization's Appeal

One of the strengths of personalization is the ability to provide services for patrons and users, effectively taking care of things for them (Montgomery and Smith 2009). A library that sends new students a virtual "care package" during the week before school begins, with information and links to resources relevant to their specific classes, would be using personalization to cut down on the amount of independent research and work students will have to do later. Students who receive this message and use the linked resources will now not have to spend as much time searching for various databases and can get started on their coursework right away.

Similarly, a library orientation for new undergraduates might split them into groups by intended major and provide each group with a scavenger hunt that helps them find databases, people, and resources relevant to their needs. Although organizing such an event would necessarily be more complicated than hosting one generic orientation, it could also help the library connect more directly with the needs of its patrons. At the same time, an activity that is personalized in this way wouldn't necessarily be of as much help to students who are undeclared, or who might later decide to change their area of focus.

Montgomery and Smith, who approach personalization from a marketing standpoint, put one core idea succinctly, writing, "Personalization then is meant to eliminate tedious tasks for the customer, and allow the marketer to better identify the user's needs and goals from past behavior" (2009, 1). Aligning the outcomes of patron needs and goals can result in better engagement and can work to strengthen the relationship between patrons and their libraries.

Personalization differs from customization in that changes and adaptations to services are initiated by the provider. Whereas customization allows users to make their own changes (think of decorated mortarboard hats at a graduation), personalized changes are those that are made based on what a library, company, or other service knows about its audience. A personalized mortarboard might be sized appropriately to a particular graduate, for example, or made of material that breathes easily for graduates in warm climates. It might even be provided automatically late in the semester before graduation in order to anticipate the need for it later. It is easy, then, to see how personalization of products and services can fit within the realm of gamification or game events in libraries: personalization allows libraries to meet patrons exactly where they are in terms of a specific service and thus allows for more connection and potentially higher engagement. In other words, personalization has the potential to help your patrons connect even more with your activity and might actually limit these students in their knowledge of relevant library services.

Names and Other Personal Identifiers

Depending on how it is carried out, personalization can also draw on deep psychological connections between attachment and identity. Numerous studies have explored the varying importance given to names by individuals—names literally define us, standing in as placeholders for us on paper, in records, in conversation. Why else would there be such a market for children's books that include a child's name? (Put Me in the Story, of www.putmeinthestory.com, has an entire line of books ready to be tailored to individual children and adults.) The frequency of studies carried out to examine the life impact of names on their holders suggests that many believe there is a profound connection between individuals and their given or adopted names (Joubert 1993).

Names in particular are salient to this discussion because of how relatively easy they are to incorporate into various efforts. Numerous websites include personalized login information, often welcoming visitors by name at the top of the page. Marketing efforts as well often incorporate names, notably in form letters and e-mails that purport to warmly greet their recipients. Writing in *Lodging Today*, Tom McCarthy describes working in a restaurant where staff who recognized customers would tip off other servers so that they could greet the customers by name. Because the customers didn't know how the staff knew them, they were often pleasantly surprised. "It's a mark of respect when a person calls you by your name," McCarthy writes. "The person went to the trouble of remembering your name and using it" (2005, 30). He also cites another restaurant that closed down in his neighborhood, speculating that he couldn't remember the staff there ever appearing to recognize him. Though these stories are anecdotal, they reflect the importance that many people place on names. While it may or may not be true that the restaurant in McCarthy's neighborhood closed down because it failed to recognize frequent customers, it is easy to also acknowledge that name recognition can go a long way toward making people feel more seen.

Personalization and Choice

One way to incorporate personalization in a game-oriented setting is by allowing players or participants to make their own choices in the context of the game's world. Think of the popularity of Choose Your Own Adventure books published by Bantam Books during the 1980s and 1990s—although the terms of these books were set by their writers, who determined every possible outcome, readers got to decide what order they would go in as they read and how their experience would progress. This decision-making process made the books different from others—the story readers encountered would vary according to what they wanted to do at any particular juncture. In addition, this encouraged repeat readings because there were so many varied possibilities. Essentially, the aspect of choice turned reading into an interactive game.

Carli Spina, writing about gamification efforts in libraries, notes that the choices that can be afforded by personalization in a game setting can be integral to establishing a connection with a patron:

> Gamified systems can also have the flexibility to permit players to choose their own approach to the game. This can be illustrated with the example of badges in any number of games. Often it would be almost impossible for players to earn every available badge and few, if any, players try to do so. Instead players identify the badges that are relevant to them or fit with their interests and pursue those. . . . This flexibility and the element of individual choice is key to making the experience meaningful for a range of participants and enriching the participants' experience with the system. (2014, 64)

Meaning is a key point here. One strength of allowing player choice in activities is that it allows greater ownership—players are putting pieces of themselves into a game or activity by embedding their choices. It should be noted that in Spina's example, the opportunity for personalization, while guided by the patron, has been set in advance by the activity's designer. This can allow a player to have a more specific, tailored experience than might be possible in a more linearly constructed activity, and it allows them to connect more directly with the goals of the project.

Examples of Projects and Activities That Incorporate Personalization

There are various ways in which personalization efforts can be incorporated into library services, both in connection with gamification and not. While some personalization efforts focus their attention on adapting a library's website to meet the needs of individual users, others use patron choice and rewards to drive activities.

Digital badges, which celebrate accomplishments that take place anywhere in a user's life—and allow them to use game elements like rewards to designate the areas they personally find important and meaningful—have also gained in momentum and are suitable for use across a spectrum of events and services. Although some of the examples listed here do not include specifically game-oriented activities, there are rich opportunities available to weave together personalization and gamification as you plan. This section will discuss a few library personalization examples that may serve as inspiration.

MyLibrary at North Carolina State University Libraries

MyLibrary, developed at North Carolina State University libraries, and adapted for use at libraries of other universities as well, including the University of Notre Dame, relies on patrons to select their discipline, and on librarians to organize resources into three categories: databases, electronic texts, and links to library resources. "More than anything else," writes Eric Lease Morgan, who worked to develop MyLibrary, "MyLibrary is intended to provide a framework for creating relationships between information resources and people" (Morgan 2008, 13).

Patrons can also add bookmarks and other associated disciplines they are interested in, which would then appear on their page. MyLibrary incorporates aspects of customization as well, allowing patrons to make changes to their page design. MyLibrary's success stems largely from its ability to cut down on work for patrons: rather than wading through seas of resources, they are able to maintain a tight focus on what might be most relevant to them. After its development, MyLibrary was released as open source software and installed in other libraries, some of which used the whole concept, and some of which selected aspects they wanted to use.

Librarygame

Librarygame (http://librarygame.co.uk/), developed by Running in the Halls Limited, works with libraries to add game-like aspects to library management systems. Patrons register to participate and link their library cards and then receive points and rewards such as badges for the work they do in the library. This is possible because Librarygame tracks patron activity, which patrons agree to allow when they sign up.

Librarygame's success hinges on rewarding people for things they are already doing and on encouraging them to engage further with a library's website and services. Like many other games, it builds over time. Patrons can see the results of their activities and do not have to spend a lot of extra time or energy in setting up gameplay or traveling to attend events. Librarygame lauds patrons for completing tasks that they could already be reasonably expected to want to complete. In a section of the Librarygame website called Why It's Awesome, Librarygame explains that it "creates an engaging, compelling and meaningful library experience for patrons of all ages. It does this while enriching your library with user generated content like reviews and ratings to help patrons choose items they love and discover things they wouldn't otherwise find" (Running in the Halls 2015). The service's focus on mutually beneficial outcomes for patrons and libraries, and its voluntary nature, may help explain its appeal, as does its attempt to provide a more interesting context for activities (such as searching catalogs, returning books, etc.) that many people do not find inherently pleasurable. Because Librarygame focuses on making patrons' real lives reflect game elements, it is able to add a degree of fun to their use of the library.

Library Involvement in the Science Learning Community at Kent State University

Librarians at Kent State University were able to become members of an already-established Science Learning Community made up of first-generation college students majoring in science-related fields (Eschedor Voelker 2006). As a part of this community, librarians attended social events, visited classes taken by Learning Community members, provided tailored library instruction and special sessions, and emphasized the library's Personalized Research Consultations (PERCS), which meant that students would meet librarians they could work with early in the semester and reach out to them specifically for information. Personalization, in this case, focused on responding to the students as a group with related interests rather than on collecting information about individuals. Student response to these efforts was largely positive, and students indicated that they wanted even more personalization than had been provided by the initiative.

Choose Your Own Adventure Summer Reading Program at the Door County Library in Sturgeon Bay, Wisconsin

Librarians in Sturgeon Bay encouraged middle-school students to read anything that interested them and record how long they read on a card they called a "passport to adventure." When students reached five hours of reading, they turned in their passports at the library to be placed in a drawing to win an adventure. Adventures included things like a ropes-challenge camp, and outings with bands, area vets, and the Coast Guard. Students could also earn reading time by volunteering at the library, and they won a book after ten hours of reading. Reactions to the initiative were largely positive, with students getting excited about the possible adventures and encouraging others to get involved (Langby 1999). Because students were able to direct the types of materials they read, they were able to make a personal connection to reading while at the same time learning new things that interested them.

Digital Badges

Digital badges can be used in many fields and contexts, and they offer a way to reward patrons for attaining various skill-sets. Hearkening back to Boy Scout and Girl Scout sashes full of colorful, tangible badges, digital badges provide tailored information and allow the recognition of nontraditional skills as well as more conventional ones. Though these skills can be academically focused, they can just as easily not be. Mozilla Open Badges (http://openbadges.org/) offers various resources for the display of digital badges. Mozilla Open Badges allows users to create a badge "backpack" that they can use as a platform for highlighting their skills through badges. These badges can celebrate anything, from learning to tie your shoes to winning a competitive grant for funding a project. More detailed information about what the badge is celebrating can be bundled with the visuals and included as part of the package (Mozilla Foundation 2012). Additionally, there are a variety of badge creation sites on the Internet.

Sheryl Grant writes, "Learning does happen anywhere, anytime, but *recognition* of that learning does not. The learning we do in museums, libraries, and on the Web can and does enrich us, but the knowledge and skills we gain are rarely recognized. Badges for learning are designed to change that" (2014, 28). Because badges are so highly adaptable, they can be tailored to particular circumstances, from instruction to outreach, and can provide recipients with a high degree of information about their learning as they progress through life. In "Open Badges for Lifelong Learning," a working document authored by the Mozilla Foundation and Peer 2 Peer University, in collaboration with the MacArthur Foundation, the authors advocate for badges in certain areas (especially those that already incorporate stringent standards) to be rigorously vetted, emphasizing that this will give the badges more value. However, the adaptability of badges means that some can also be awarded for less formal pursuits and might adhere to different criteria (2012).

In "Badging a Conference," Fontichiaro et al. discuss the experience of providing badges to be distributed by vendors and presenters at the 2012 Ohio Educational Library Media Association (OELMA) conference. They report that the reaction was "a mix of excitement, suspicion, curiosity, and hesitation" (2013, 6), but that many colleagues seemed to very much enjoy the experience of gaining badges that rewarded them for learning, and they were able to start valuable discussions that they might not have been able to have otherwise. Providing digital badges at events such as orientations, tabling sessions, and outreach events is one way in which librarians can think about incorporating more game elements into their services in a voluntary and relatively unobtrusive way. Because these badges reflect the learning and accomplishments of the individuals who hold them, they are a good example of how personalized game elements can succeed in the right context.

Digital badges clearly reflect a growing interest in both game elements (by rewarding people using a specified system when they meet their goals) and personalization. Because digital badges do not correspond directly to any particular field of study or set of information, they allow users to celebrate what is important to them and to define what that is for themselves. Digital badges can let users set their own goals and take a more active role in the design of their own learning.

⑥ Personalization Concerns

In 2011, Eli Pariser delivered a TED talk about the dangers of what he calls "filter bubbles"—ways in which information that people find online becomes curated to match their interests. Though this can be beneficial in some ways—for instance, in allowing people to connect more readily with the information that is most relevant to them—in his talk, Pariser outlines ways in which he believes it can also be very harmful.

When people only see information that matches their interests, they can develop worldviews and understandings that do not reflect reality. Pariser illustrates this by showing two Google searches conducted by different people on the same topic, side by side. Pariser had asked both searchers to conduct a search about Egypt, using the same search terms. One search completely eliminated information about the protests and unrest in

Egypt that were at that time dominating the news, and it focused instead on travel options and historical background. This searcher's search history was effectively determining their interests for them and depriving them of major news. The other search included information about the protests and unrest, which meant that this searcher, by virtue of their past history, was getting more information about current events. Filter bubbles can work to isolate people from important information across the political spectrum and can prevent them from having rational discussions (Pariser 2011).

Others have noted difficulty in replicating Pariser's experiment—Jacob Weisberg (2011), writing in *Slate*, for example, asked five politically diverse friends and acquaintances to do searches with terms such as "Obamacare" and "John Boehner" and found that differences in the results of their searches were negligible. Whether or not filter bubbles are, in fact a cause for concern, the issue of personalization is one to consider carefully before you decide to use it in a game or activity.

Apart from concerns about getting the best information, personalization can also cause users to become suspicious of the intentions of a service provider, which can work to erode trust. In *The Dark Side of Personalization*, Jörg Ziesak reports that informing users of an intention to collect information makes them more worried about the reasons you have for doing this. Furthermore, Ziesak writes, "the more users are concerned, the less value they see in the advantages of personalization and the more risk is perceived" (2013, 29). Aguirre et al. back this up, referring to it as "the personalization paradox" (2015). While Ziesak and Aguirre et al. are reporting on the use of personalization in business settings, there are clear parallels to work in library settings. Perhaps even more than in marketing scenarios, library patrons count on their libraries to provide trustworthy, solid information.

Privacy

Libraries have long worked to protect patron privacy, and, despite its advantages from a relationship-building perspective, personalization can also erode trust. Coming back to the Amazon book suggestion example from earlier, a reader may ask, "But how does Amazon *know* I might be interested in those books? What do they know about me? Why do they want me to look at these specific items?"

William Badke writes that "personalization can serve two possible interests: first, our own desire to customize whatever tool we are using to best meet our search needs, and second, the intention of vendors to target their goods to our preferences" (2012, 47). Badke is critical of personalization, finding it to be of pressing concern for researchers and students who may be limited by overly targeted information that purports to take the place of more honest research findings. He is not alone in this view.

Although the root of personalization is the ability to get to know and understand patrons and customers, the methods by which information about them is unearthed can make a difference in how an activity is received. Aguirre et al. refer to two different types of information collection strategies: overt and covert (2015). In overt strategies, an attempt is made to inform participants that information about them is being collected, usually by some kind of notification posted on a website or a sign. Covert information collection, which is popular on the Internet for its seamlessness, allows the collection of data without informing participants beforehand. Aguirre et al. note that covert information collection "benefits consumers, by not interfering with their surfing experience" (2015, 36).

Benefits and Drawbacks

There is evidence indicating that some level of personalization encourages users (in this case, retail consumers) to engage more with products and services. On the other hand, there is also evidence that too much personalization makes people worry that their privacy may have been violated. Aguirre et al. conducted a study that asked participants in two groups to first read an article about Facebook's use of user data (either an article emphasizing Facebook's data collection or one that said Facebook users were unaware of data collection used to create advertisements) and then answer questions about whether they would click on an ad seen through Facebook. They also responded to a survey about how the ad made them feel. Aguirre et al. discuss the results of their study:

> In some conditions, personalization leads to greater click-through intentions; specifically, and consistent with our prediction, more personalization increases click-through intentions when firms overtly collect consumer data to provide personalized services. When firms covertly collect data though, consumers feel more vulnerable when they realize their information has been collected without their permission, which decreases their click-through intentions. (2015, 41)

Although gamification efforts in libraries may not rely on click-throughs in order to structure activity, the bigger concern may be not to overwhelm patrons or treat their privacy callously. In a world populated by billboards, targeted mailings, and curiously knowledgeable form e-mails, overly aggressive strategies may backfire, in addition to being ethically suspect.

Near the end of his 2001 book *Making It Personal: How to Profit from Personalization without Invading Privacy*, Bruce Kasanoff nicely summarizes both what can be troubling about personalization, and what can be exciting:

> Personalization is about people, and the things that matter most to them, which, as we've already discussed, progresses from basic to higher-order needs. The ultimate payoff of personalization has to be that it enables us to help each other, because that's the behavior that emerges at the top of the ladder. (2001, 182)

It is easy to lose sight of the impact of a meaningful personal connection when faced with so many ways that personalization can go wrong, but if done right—and in moderation—it can be a unique tool to build connections between libraries and their patrons. Although at first it can be tempting to use knowledge of patron interests and desires to reach out, attempts to tailor events and services to users' needs and goals should be approached gingerly, and with a healthy respect for privacy.

Personalizing the Library Stars Tour

The Library Stars Tour, like many games, may be difficult to personalize completely. Although some elements of personalization, such as choice, are integrated into the tour already, there are avenues for further personalization as well if it appears that this would help the game connect with students. How could this be done? Possible avenues for personalization include

- Questions adapted to the needs of particular classes or faculty members. (There are some knots that could arise here, from workload considerations to potential communication problems, but benefits include a closer connection with a faculty member and a class and potentially more student buy-in and engagement.)
- Developing a digital badge system that can be completed by patrons who want to earn library incentives or increase their knowledge of library services. (The Library Stars Tour could, under this umbrella, become one of many tasks that students could complete and display as a personal accomplishment.)
- Choice of reward at the end of the activity. (Depending on partnerships you develop outside the library, it is possible to provide options for rewards. This affords players more choice and makes the incentive potentially more meaningful for them.)

Although the potential audience for this particular game is large, players should not feel like they are being herded through it, especially since one of the game's objectives is to make the library a more familiar and comfortable place for students. Providing small choices and personalization options, even if they end up being more time-consuming in the short run, can be helpful ways to build relationships.

⊚ Key Points

This chapter has focused on how personalization of services and activities may be beneficial to patrons in your library as you design and hone gamification efforts. Not every game-related activity needs to incorporate a large degree of personalization, but there can be advantages to weaving some strands of personalization and patron choice into your overall project. At the same time, it is crucial not to violate patrons' privacy and to be as transparent as possible in your use of personal identifiers and information.

- Personalization can be a good way to forge connections between your library and your patrons because

  - It can reduce work for patrons
  - It can help patrons drive their own learning in the library
  - It provides options for interaction and encourages flexibility

- Personalized services in a library setting may take the form of face-to-face time with affinity groups, tailored learning management systems, and digital badges, among other options.
- In spite of its advantages, personalization also has the capacity to hurt library relationships with patrons and to deprive patrons of the information that they need. If you decide to add aspects of personalization to your game efforts, you will want to proceed with caution.
- Personalization is not only possible in the Library Stars Tour game. It could also serve as a venue for the development of stronger relationships with outside stakeholders, for example, by customizing game questions to particular groups or classes, or by situating the game in the context of a badge patrons can receive for completing various library tasks.

In the next chapter, you will learn about strategies to use when setting goals and objectives for your project.

References

Aguirre, Elizabeth, Dominik Mahr, Dhruv Grewal, Ko de Ruyter, and Martin Wetzels. 2015. "Unraveling the Personalization Paradox: The Effect of Information Collection and Trust-Building Strategies on Online Advertisement Effectiveness." *Journal of Retailing* 91 (1): 34–49.

Badke, William. 2012. "Personalization and Information Literacy." *Online* 36 (1): 47–49.

Eschedor Voelker, Tammy J. 2006. "The Library and My Learning Community: First Year Student's Impressions of Library Services." *Reference & User Services Quarterly* 46 (2): 72–80.

Fontichiaro, Kristin et al. 2013. "Badging a Conference." *School Library Monthly* 29 (7): 5–7.

Grant, Sheryl. 2014. "Badges: Show What You Know." *Young Adult Library Services* 12 (2): 28–32.

Joubert, Charles C. E. 1993. "Personal Names as a Psychological Variable." *Psychological Reports* 73 (2): 1123–45.

Kasanoff, Bruce. 2001. *Making It Personal: How to Profit from Personalization without Invading Privacy.* Cambridge, MA: Perseus Publishing.

Langby, Leah. 1999. "Adventure Stories." *School Library Journal* 45 (11): 35.

McCarthy, Tom. 2005. "It's All in a Name." *Lodging Hospitality* 61 (2): 30.

Montgomery, Alan L., and Michael D. Smith. 2009. "Prospects for Personalization on the Internet." *Journal of Interactive Marketing* 23 (2): 130–37.

Morgan, Eric Lease. 2008. "MyLibrary: A Digital Library Framework and Toolkit." *Information Technology & Libraries* 27 (3): 12–24.

Mozilla Foundation, Peer 2 Peer University, and the MacArthur Foundation. 2012. "Open Badges for Lifelong Learning: Exploring an Open Badge Ecosystem to Support Skill Development and Lifelong Learning for Real Results Such as Jobs and Advancement." https://wiki.mozilla.org/images/b/b1/OpenBadges-Working-Paper_092011.pdf.

Pariser, Eli. 2011. "TED Talks Eli Pariser—Beware Online 'Filter Bubbles.'" www.ted.com/talks/eli_pariser_beware_online_filter_bubbles?language=en.

Running in the Halls. 2015. "Why Librarygame Is Awesome." Librarygame. http://librarygame.co.uk/why.html.

Spina, Carli. 2014. "Gamification in Libraries." In *Games in Libraries*, edited by Breanne A. Kirsch, 62–79. Jefferson, NC: McFarland & Company.

Weisberg, Jacob. 2011. "Bubble Trouble: Is Web Personalization Turning Us Into Solipsistic Twits?" *Slate*. www.slate.com/articles/news_and_politics/the_big_idea/2011/06/bubble_trouble.html.

Ziesak, Jörg. 2013. "The Dark Side of Personalization Online Privacy Concerns Influence Customer Behavior." Hamburg, Germany: Anchor Academic Publishing.

Setting Goals and Objectives

THIS CHAPTER WILL DISCUSS strategies for setting goals and objectives as you start to plan your project. Largely, the planning that you do in preparation for your project will depend on your library, what you are hoping to get from the project and the specific demographics at your library. If you are just beginning to dip your feet into the waters of gamification, you may experiment a bit before diving in all the way, and that is fine. Games at the library can encompass a wide number of types of projects, from intensive scavenger hunts that happen one time per semester to ongoing projects that link patron borrowing information to rewards, so necessarily, much of the nuts-and-bolts planning that you do will depend on your activity and what you are hoping to get from it. That being said, thoughtful coordination and attention can help you set and plan toward desired goals and outcomes, which can give your project a better chance at success.

Setting achievable goals, thinking analytically about the various aspects of what you are working on, and focusing on the needs of your audience will help to steer your project. Perhaps counter-intuitively, it can be beneficial to plan less around the determination of goals to be met for your library, and more around the determination of goals you can help your patrons meet for themselves while they participate. Especially in a library setting, where no one is obligated to engage in outreach projects and initiatives, appealing to autonomy is essential.

There may also be other considerations—for example, whether you will add elements of gamification to an existing service, or develop an entirely new project. You will need to think carefully about the services you offer and how to add to them or complement them. This may involve thinking critically about who uses your library and what their needs and motivations might be. Whatever you decide to plan will need to fit comfortably with your other offerings and services, and spending some time thinking through ideas and fleshing out your objectives will prove valuable in the long run.

Planning and critical thinking can help you craft a more streamlined and effective activity. The decisions you make and ideas you have in the very earliest stages of this process will help to ensure that your final project is both successful and a great framework to build on in the future.

⊚ Developing the Breadth of Your Project

One of the first decisions you may make as you begin to think about incorporating gamification elements into your services has to do with the scope of your project. Will you add game elements to an existing service? Or will you instead develop something totally new? Librarians have worked with both models to create successful, game-inspired experiences for their patrons. Below are examples of two projects—one that builds off an existing service, and one that creates an entirely new experience for library patrons.

Working with Existing Services

Lemontree, Running in the Halls' Librarygame variety in use at the University of Huddersfield, uses information from linked patron library cards to reward the cards' users for using the library (Running in the Halls 2015). It builds on basic library services, like allowing users to check out materials and work with databases. Actions like returning books, visiting the library, and using electronic resources award points to users. The game includes a visual progress bar and allows users to connect with friends as they work on their research.

Leaderboards and information on how users from different schools stack up against each other add to the sense of friendly competition. On Librarygame blog, Lemontree's creators discuss some of their thinking in designing the game:

- Library interfaces are usually unattractive and clunky; it's important for first year students to gravitate towards something that looks new and is constantly being refined. Aesthetically pleasing designs look easier to use and have a higher probability of being used constantly.
- There is a social layer that helps students filter the half a million books at the library and learn together. If you know what your fellow course members are studying and looking at, you're more likely to find out more about the kind of things you could borrow. Same goes with Ratings, allowing recommendations between users and so on.
- Profiling desired behavior. In academia as with any other situation where social proof is a powerful force, there's a definite sense that signposting and making visible scholarly activity and leaving a trace of it has a desirable effect. (Running in the Halls 2011)

Lemontree's success seems to stem (at least in part) from its reliance on enhancing the research experiences of people who are already using the library. It rewards people for doing something that they (hopefully) are already doing: using the library and library services to complete the work they need to get done for their classes and research.

The blog post also reveals some other considerations that you may wish to keep in mind as you think about developing a game experience. In their first bullet point, they identify an issue with many library websites and interfaces—in effect, they are using what they see as an aesthetic flaw as a jumping off point. Attention to the reactions and emotional responses of their audience allows them to create something more appealing. At the same time, by incorporating social aspects into their service, Lemontree helps students learn from each other, weaving in the conversations students are having anyway about the library and giving them a predetermined venue. Lastly, and most ostensibly in line with library goals for students, the game promotes a behavior that the school and the library want: student use of library facilities and services. Overall, participants in Lemontree are getting something that they want from it: rewards, a chance to socialize, and a healthy outlet for their competitive impulses. Lemontree more indirectly meets possible library goals by encouraging patrons to use the library more frequently than they might otherwise, and to check out and return materials, but these are not the primary areas of patron focus.

This project has the added benefit of fitting into the grooves of established practices at the University of Huddersfield. The library was already providing the services that form the root of the activities Lemontree users complete—Lemontree just provided rewards and a place for students to engage in friendly competition. This means that Lemontree does not work in conflict with anything else that is happening in the library. The overall effect is of a seamless flow.

Developing a New Experience

Having an existing activity or service to springboard off of is not essential when you are thinking about a project, however. In *Knowing When to Create a Library Game*, Mary J. Snyder Broussard, a librarian at Snowden Library of Lycoming College, discusses a Harry Potter night she developed with her colleagues featuring "themed food, bowtruckle hunts, crafts, costume contests, Quidditch toss, potions making, and obstacle courses" (Snyder Broussard 2014, 32). They identified broad objectives that focused on appealing to students, specifically, "to involve students with an interest in this hugely popular series and to show the library and its staff in a positive way" (2014, 32). The game was held for several years, and it garnered a good amount of participation. Participating students seemed to enjoy the event, with Snyder Broussard recalling that one first-year student told her, "This is the most fun I've had so far at college!" (2014, 32). Although this game wasn't explicitly designed to teach students about the library, it turned the library into a welcoming space that really thinks about its patrons. Since the event stemmed from an existing student interest in the books, its design reflected an attention to students and a desire to help them. In a small community (Lycoming has 1,400 students), this attention to patron needs in the form of an opportunity to socialize and celebrate a popular book series would most likely be much appreciated. It is also highly probable that students who feel more comfortable using the library thanks to this event will be more likely to come back when they need help with their research.

While the two projects discussed above are different, they both underline how attention to patron needs and issues can have a positive impact for students and patrons alike. As you consider adding gamification elements to your library, you may want to consider a few questions.

- What interests do your patrons have?
- Is there a particular service you would like to enhance?

- Will your project be ongoing or a one-time event?
- Does your project reflect patron interests or make the library a more welcoming place?

Thinking about these questions will help you plan your project, whether you decide to gamify an existing service or to instead develop a standalone event. They will also help you keep focused on the needs and desires of your patrons, and this focus should drive your work to incorporate game elements. Since gamification is primarily about making time at the library more interesting, engaging, and enjoyable for patrons, make sure that your project reflects what is important to them.

ⓖ Defining Success

Once you know that you are interested in incorporating elements of gamification into your library, you will need to think about what you are hoping to gain from doing so, both for yourself and for your patrons. Consider the following scenario.

Katie, a librarian at a mid-size public library, is designing a scavenger hunt to tell her patrons more about library services. She is hoping that a fun, upbeat event will attract people who aren't frequent library users and will help her regular patrons get excited about the various opportunities available at the library. She maps out a varied and interesting route through the library, engages her colleagues to help give out clues and coordinate hints, and spends a weekend putting up flyers around town and posting announcements on the library's social media page. However, on the day of the event, only four people arrive to participate. Katie can't help but feel disappointed. After all, she did so much work, and it only benefitted four people.

Later on, when Katie reads evaluation surveys, she sees that the patrons who participated had a great time and felt like they learned a lot about the library. They say they appreciated her effort and will come back in the future to use library services. But Katie still feels let down. Though it seems like the event was a success for the people who participated, she had been hoping it would have a bigger impact.

Part of the issue with Katie's project is that she did not decide early in the planning process what success with her project might look like. Thus, it became difficult for her to know whether or not it was a success. Deciding what is important to you and how you want to use it to build toward the future will give you a sense of what you are looking for as you begin to plan your project.

Additionally—and more pragmatically—for better or worse, many libraries are in the position of needing to justify the ways they spend money. Therefore, more and more there is an emphasis in libraries on return on investment (ROI). Put simply, this is the idea that libraries (and businesses and other venues), should not be money pits that produce nothing. ROI is a method that can be used to evaluate whether or not a library is performing in a way that demonstrates value. ROI is about money and whether it is worth it to spend money on various projects.

In *Applying Return on Investment (ROI) in Libraries*, Betsy Kelly, Claire Hamasu, and Barbara Jones argue that libraries must be able to demonstrate in calculated ways that they have value: "In the current economic climate competition for resources justifies employing ROI both for demonstrating the value the library adds to the organization and for supporting budget requests" (2012, 669). Your library may not put a heavy emphasis on ROI as a direct method for measurement of success, but it is still a useful tool to keep in mind.

As you think about success for your project, you may want to consider what kind of value it will bring to your library, whether that is in terms of money or not. Although it can be fun to think of projects such as theme days or potlucks or board game nights (and none of these are bad ideas), it is also essential to understand why you are planning a project or event to begin with, and what success with that project or event will entail.

⊚ Establishing Goals and Outcomes

Establishing goals for your project is one of the ways you will be able to tell whether or not it was a success. There are many different ways to think about your goals for a project, and success doesn't always look the same. In some ways, this is like running a race. If your goal is to be the first person across the finish line, then you might be discouraged if someone else finishes first. But if your goal is just to reach the end of the race, you might be elated as you sail beneath the finishing-line balloons. Neither one of these outcomes is inherently better or worse—they are just different ways of thinking about what you want to accomplish, what you feel prepared to accomplish, and what you will eventually be able to do.

Your library and your patrons will, in large part, help to shape your goal. You may—and probably will—have different motivations at an academic library than at a public library because these two spaces can have very different patrons, missions, and services. In a school library, your goals might focus on getting children excited to read, for instance, while at a public library you may focus more on outreach and service to the community. In an academic or school library, you may need to focus on how your project fits with the established curriculum as well. If your goal is just to get more people to walk in the door of the library, an event that boosts attendance might succeed beautifully, even if those same people don't end up producing intricately researched projects afterward. Bohyun Kim, associate director for library applications and knowledge systems at the University of Maryland Health Sciences and Human Services Library, points out that gamification's newness as a tool for libraries means that many game-related projects do not in fact have clear goals (2015). That being said, determining which aspects of your project are the most important can be useful.

> Suppose that an instructor gamifies part of or all homework for a class with a leaderboard, points, teams, challenges, missions, and badges. The goal of this gamification may simply be to increase the number of students who submit the homework on time. Or the goal can be set as better grades from the students in the low performance group, the longer retention time of the subject knowledge taught, or increasing students' collaboration skills through working out challenges and missions as a team. Setting a clear goal for a gamification project makes it much easier to design the project and to evaluate it after it is run. (Kim 2015, 32)

The goals mentioned above may seem simple—encouraging students to turn in homework on time is nothing new in educational settings. But gamification can help make this everyday process of completing and turning in homework a more pleasurable experience that allows students and teachers to work together more effectively. Even simple goals that hinge directly on key outcomes for a project or service can both assist in assessment and help you determine whether or not your project was successful.

Goals in various areas have at least one thing in common: they need to focus on patrons. In *Drive: The Surprising Truth About What Motivates Us*, Daniel Pink reports on the work of Edward Deci and Richard Ryan, who developed the idea of "self-determination theory" (Pink 2009, 71). This theory is driven by the idea that at their core, people want to be "autonomous, self-determined, and connected to one another" (2009, 73). This applies to your patrons. Although as a librarian, you may think about goals and success from the standpoint of your organization, if you want your project to be successful, you need to frame it around the people who will take part and their personal motivations. It is crucial to think about why your project is going to be helpful in some way to the people who will be its participants.

Consider the Lemontree interactive game again. Students who participate in the game are not really being asked to do anything out of the ordinary in the course of their library research. They already know they will probably need to use the library in order to be successful students. But the fact that they can earn rewards and compete with each other as they go about their daily lives adds extra incentive and encourages them to be more involved. Even a game that you think would be fundamentally interesting and helpful to patrons is not going to appeal to them unless you can take into consideration their motivations and reasons for participation.

In *Gamify: How Gamification Motivates People to Do Extraordinary Things*, Brian Burke discusses a seeming contradiction in many gamification endeavors: organizations want to implement gamified projects so that they can meet their own goals, but gamified projects will only really work if they reflect the goals of their participants:

> One of the key problems in many gamified solutions is that they are focused on getting players to achieve the organization's goals rather than players' goals. Gamified solutions must put players' motivations and goals first and make them the primary design objective. This player-centric design approach is not intuitive, but every design decision must be focused on motivating players and enabling them to be successful in achieving their goals and ambitions. The solution must build a series of challenges that engages the players at an emotional level and motivates them to achieve a goal that is meaningful to them. (2014, 21)

Since the participants are the heart of your project, any goals that you set for the project must also take into consideration the goals that they have for themselves. People want to be independent—they want to be able to decide the course of their own lives. Ignoring this aspect when adding game elements to library services will most likely result in less participation and reduced impact. Though the goals that you set as a librarian will necessarily take into consideration the specific accomplishments you would like to attain for the library, you will also need to work to align these goals with those of your potential audience.

Goal-Setting Basics

As you begin to work specifically at targeting your goals, there are a few things that may be helpful to keep in mind. To start, goals don't need to be long and complicated. They can be simple statements that reflect what you would like patrons to get out of your activity and what you are hoping to achieve. Edwin A. Locke and Gary P. Latham found that specific, high (hard) goals lead to a higher level of task performance than do easy goals or vague, abstract goals such as the exhortation to "do one's best." So long as a person is committed to the goal, has the requisite ability to attain it, and does not have conflicting goals, there is a positive, linear relationship between goal difficulty and task performance. (2006, 265)

Using these findings as guidance, it can be beneficial to focus on just a few goals at one time—after all, an activity that is designed to teach every patron every possible thing about using libraries is probably doomed to fail in at least some part of its mission. Goals should be clear and specific, and it should be possible to figure out whether they have been met. Goals that have too many moving parts may be difficult to really assess. A goal like "Users will understand library databases" may be impossible to truly assess. Who can know what or how much another human really understands about something?

Locke and Latham also emphasize the need to focus on goals that move learners closer to the understanding of concepts and ideas, rather than goals focusing on attaining the big picture. "Focusing on reaching a specific performance outcome on a new complex task can lead to 'tunnel vision,'" they write, "a focus on reaching the goal rather than ac-quiring the skills required to reach it. In such cases the best results are attained if a learn-ing goal is assigned—that is a goal to acquire the requisite task knowledge" (2006, 266).

Carol Dweck, a Stanford University psychology professor, also believes in the power of goals that emphasize growth and learning. Her research considers two different ways of looking at goals. She identifies them as "fixed" and "growth" mindsets, writing that

these two mindsets lead to different school behaviors. For one thing, when students view intelligence as fixed, they tend to value looking smart above all else. They may sacrifice important opportunities to learn—even those that are important to their future academic success—if those opportunities require them to risk performing poorly or admitting defi-ciencies. Students with a growth mindset, on the other hand, view challenging work as an opportunity to learn and grow. I have seen students with a growth mindset meet difficult problems, ones they could not solve yet, with a great relish. (2010, 1)

Pulling this research together, it becomes clear that specific goals that value learning and growth can be helpful to both you and your patrons as you craft and shape your project. You will want to emphasize that the steps of your project are a way patrons can develop, rather than signposts to be slapped as they run past. Working carefully to hone and refine your objectives for patrons and to ensure that these are in line with their own goals for their library experience can be very rewarding.

In this same vein, thinking critically about who your patrons are as people can also help you figure out what is important to them. You may consider the age range of your potential patrons—for example, whether they are students and at what level (high school, primary school, graduate school, etc.); their gender identification; or their culture. In an academic library at a university with a high population of commuter students, for exam-ple, you may want to tailor activities to fit their lives—potentially including online proj-ects, or projects that can be completed anytime and don't require an extra trip to campus. Even a beautifully planned event will fail if it doesn't address the realities of patrons' lives.

It may also be useful to think about how patron motivation can influence your potential participants' desire to be a part of your activity. Motivation generally is either intrinsic or extrinsic. Intrinsic motivation means motivation that comes from within—learning to play an instrument because you love the way it sounds is an example of intrinsic motivation, as is donating money to help people in need. Extrinsic motivation is a result of getting rewards—money, advancement, good grades, prestige—for something you've done. The problem is that studies suggest that extrinsic rewards can diminish peoples' drive to complete activities for their own sake (Deci, Koestner, and Ryan 1999). Because of this, you will want to think long and hard about how you will appeal to your patrons' desire to participate. Kim suggests that one way around this dilemma could be to design activities that allow users to set their own goals rather than pushing them toward your own (2015). She also explains that one-time external rewards, or rewards for completing everyday activities, may be safer since they do not rely on participants' expectation of the reward to accomplish their goals.

The important thing to take from this section is that careful consideration of your goals, your library, and your project's emotional engagement with your patrons will help you determine how successful your project is, and it is essential to have a vision of what success will look like as you start to plan. Incorporating gamification into your services and outreach is often fun, so it can be tempting just to jump in headfirst without thinking. Careful planning and a clear definition of success, however, will let you know for sure if you have reached the goals you set for your project.

◎ Starting at the End

When people say that hindsight is 20/20, they usually aren't talking about planning events in a library. That being said, this common phrase can easily be applied to many sorts of long-range planning projects, both in and out of the library, and thinking about goals before you're close to accomplishing them can help you reach them more effectively. More importantly, it will help you think strategically and analytically about the various pieces of your project so that they add up to a cohesive experience for patrons. Planning what you hope to get from your project can contribute to the success of the event as a whole.

The principle of *backward design* can be of assistance as you plan for what you are hoping to accomplish. In short, backward design is about starting at the end: by thinking about what you want the finish line to look like, you can work to ensure that the road your patrons will take to get there is the right one—or at least is going in the right direction. In *Understanding by Design* (2005), Grant P. Wiggins and Jay McTighe identify three stages of backward design:

1. Identify desired results.
2. Determine acceptable evidence.
3. Plan learning experiences and instruction.

These three stages help to break down what can at first seem like a daunting and monumental task. By identifying what you are hoping to accomplish and then deciding how you will know you have accomplished it, you are charting a course for yourself that will help guide your project.

When Wiggins and McTighe discuss results, they break this down further by mapping out a framework that helps determine which results will take priority over others in the course of planning. They consider these priorities and focus sharply on the most important goals by considering knowledge in three areas: What is worth knowing about, What is important to know about, and What are the big ideas or core tasks in an area

(2005, 71). Homing in on what is most important about your project will help as you think about what you want your patrons to do and know as a result of the activity. Depending on the amount of time available and on the context of the audience and project, you may choose to focus your attention on all three of these areas to some degree, or you may maintain a focus just on the big ideas. You may not draw up plans in this mold for every activity you create, but having an idea of what might be important can still be helpful.

Once you decide where to focus your goals, it may be comforting to realize that you most likely don't need to use your project to teach every single patron every single thing about everything that is good to know in your library. In "How Do Our Students Learn? An Outline of a Cognitive Psychological Model for Information Literacy Instruction," Dani Brecher Cook and Kevin Michael Klipfel discuss effective teaching from a cognitive science perspective. Although their approach is geared toward instruction in libraries and not gamification, their suggestions may be useful if you are trying to use game elements to reach patrons—and especially if you are planning to incorporate game elements in your instruction. One of their suggestions is deceptively simple: Do less. They write,

> What we call "learning" begins when information enters the working memory, the part of the brain that "holds the stuff you're thinking about" and which is the site of the information processing that is addressed in cognitive load theory. For information to be learned, it needs to travel from the working memory to the long-term memory, which stores facts and procedures for later recall. Simply put, this means that only information that fits into an individual's working memory has even a chance of being learned. (2015, 4)

From a backward design perspective, this means that it is especially important to decide which are the key elements of your project before you begin designing. Those are the ones that your project should focus on, and you may want to consider focusing a good deal of energy on these goals. Although library game efforts are not always directly tied to teaching, you may hope to impart information or inform patrons of specific services through your project. Even if nothing else about your project looks like instruction, slowing down and thinking about what is really important can help guide your planning process and get you closer to what you want to accomplish.

⑥ Critical Considerations

As you work to identify what is most important in your activity or event, you may want to spend some time thinking about your approach and what signals it might send—deliberately or inadvertently—to patrons. You also may want to think critically about the materials being used. Considering the reasons you have for asking patrons to engage in a particular activity in a specific way can help shape your plan so that the message doesn't become lost. Keeping set goals in mind can help you focus on what you want patrons to know. Wiggins and McTighe approach this idea from an educational standpoint, analyzing how a teacher might decide to use a book as part of a class.

> Why are we asking students to read this particular novel—in other words, what learnings will we seek from their having read it? Do the students grasp why and how the purpose should influence their studying? What should students be expected to understand and do upon reading the book, related to our goals beyond the book? Unless we begin our design work with a clear insight into larger purposes—whereby the book is properly thought of

as a means to an educational end, not an end unto itself—it is unlikely that all students will understand the book (and their performance obligations). (2005, 28)

Planning can encourage deeper reflection on the goals of a particular activity or project. For example, it may help to think critically about your reasons for structuring a particular event as a scavenger hunt rather than as a trivia game about library services, or as an informal social media contest. Marshall McLuhan, a Canadian philosopher, famously said, "The medium is the message," and this statement can be valuable food for thought. What are you really telling patrons if you teach them about information literacy in short nuggets on social media? How about if you are teaching them how to find research information via a scavenger hunt? Upon reflection, you may decide that you are happy with the venue you have planned, or you may choose to change it. As with most decisions at the heart of your project, it is up to you.

Planning for Your Patrons

You may have noticed that this chapter focuses mainly on large ideas to keep in mind as you think about your project. Every project is different—some will take relatively minimal planning, and some will involve an extensive amount of research, collaboration, and analysis. One common element of these projects, however, is the need to keep a razor-sharp focus on the people who really matter: your patrons. Whether your project adds game elements to some aspect of the patron experience or encourages patrons to view the library and library staff in a more favorable light, your patrons are the people who will ultimately gauge whether or not it was a success. You can help your patrons find meaning in your project by weaving in aspects that can help them accomplish their goals. As you work to develop your project, you may also want to think carefully and analytically about each step in order to determine how to best achieve results. Planning with a careful eye on your goals and those of your patrons will help your project be more successful, and ultimately will help you continue to design successful projects in the future.

Setting Goals for the Library Stars Tour

Many of the goals for the Library Stars Tour are laid out explicitly by its very nature: it is meant to introduce students to the library and to increase their comfort with asking questions and using library services. Still, it is important to evaluate each part of the tour in order to make sure that it all aligns with the stated objectives. These objectives are listed below, along with the tour components that reflect them. Major and minor objectives are listed separately. Although not all of the objectives are top priorities, all of them contribute to the experience of students participating in the activity. The major objectives are

- To familiarize students with the library
- To encourage students to see the library and library staff as resources they can use to answer questions
- To help students become more comfortable using the library
- To establish lines of communication with faculty members who do not generally bring their students to the library

TEXTBOX 3.1

TYPES OF GOALS AND QUESTIONS TO ASK

Goals in an Academic Setting

- Will this activity help students learn?
- Does this activity support some aspect of school curriculum?
- Will this activity help students become better researchers?

Attendance Goals

- Why would this activity appeal to the patrons of my library?
- What needs do my patrons have that are not being addressed yet by the library?
- What interests do my patrons have, in or outside the library?

Social Goals

- How can I make this activity fun or engaging for participants?
- How can I encourage people to work together in the activity?
- Will I ask people to work in groups? If so, will they create the groups themselves, or will I create the groups?
- Can people complete this activity on their own?

Helping Patrons Become Familiar with Services

- What library services will patrons use as they complete this activity?
- What services do I want them to know about?
- What services fit with the themes and overall goals of this activity?

More minor (but still important) objectives include

- Giving students a sense of how to use the catalog to find library materials
- Introducing students to specific spaces that are often used by undergraduate students: the circulation desk, the Media Viewing Room, the Library Reading Room, etc.
- Establishing the library as a place for fun as well as research and to remove lingering anxiety students may have about approaching library staff and asking for help

The major objectives listed at the top are ones that may seem clear from the beginning—the tour will involve students in the library, after all, and so ensuring that they familiarize themselves with it comes with the territory. However, as the planning process continues, some of the other objectives may gain importance, especially given the fact that the students who take the tour will largely not have spent much time in the library over the past semester. These various components were interwoven in the fabric of the tour in the hope that students would both begin to feel more comfortable and become more knowledgeable about library spaces and services.

The tour addresses these major and minor objectives in several ways. Students move through the library spaces, encountering various places that may be useful to them later. The autograph-book component of the tour rewards students for approaching staff members and gives them a quick conversation starter. Much emphasis in the tour is placed on student comfort—they can complete the tour on their own or with friends, and they are encouraged to enter the raffle and win prizes. The "star" theme is also rather silly, and it may suggest that students not take the tour too seriously. Also, the prizes and movie-themed giveaways underline that student downtime and relaxation are important too—though this is an academic library setting, there are plenty of resources available to students who want to come in and decompress.

Based on the goals of the Library Stars Tour, it is clear that the tour will be successful if the following occur:

- Students from most introductory writing classes complete the tour.
- Most students answer the questions correctly.
- Students obtain autographs from a variety of library staff members.
- Students indicate via surveys that they enjoyed themselves and learned about the library.
- Informal conversations with students who come in for reference assistance indicate that they remember the tour.
- Faculty members indicate via surveys that they think the tour is worthwhile.

The goals for the Library Stars Tour accomplish several objectives, including guiding tour planning and emphasis and establishing the best measures for informal tour assessment. They also serve to set the stage for other, later activities that may include the same students and faculty.

Key Points

This chapter has focused on the steps to take as you begin the planning process for your project. By carefully considering each piece of your activity and how it fits into your overall goals, you can develop an experience for patrons that allows them to learn about library services and meet their own goals at the same time.

- Success can be achieved through either a standalone project or a project that jumps off from an existing service—but you need to determine which will work best in the context of your activity and your library.
- Project success is defined by measuring results against targeted expectations that you set for the event or activity. Put simply: You will decide what a successful project looks like ahead of time and then see how well your activity measures up.
- Set goals for yourself, your activity, and your patrons, but focus on ways the activity you're planning can help patrons achieve their own goals. Goals help to maintain focus, and participants who have goals perform better than those who don't.
- Plan your project with your predetermined goals in mind.

- Think carefully about each stage of your project so that you are not inadvertently providing the wrong message.
- The Library Stars Tour's goals helped to structure the tour, establish areas of particular emphasis, and guide later assessment of its success, while at the same time establishing connections with students and faculty members.

In the next chapter, you will learn more specifically about the design process.

ⓖ References

Burke, Brian. 2014. *Gamify: How Gamification Motivates People to Do Extraordinary Things*. Brookline, MA: Bibliomotion.

Cook, Dani Brecher, and Kevin Michael Klipfel. 2015. "How Do Our Students Learn? An Outline of a Cognitive Psychological Model for Information Literacy Instruction." *Reference & User Services Quarterly* 5, no. 1.

Deci, Edward L., Richard Koestner, and Richard M. Ryan. 1999. "A Meta-Analytic Review of Experiments Examining the Effects of Extrinsic Rewards on Intrinsic Motivation." *Psychological Bulletin* 125, no. 6 (November): 627–68.

Dweck, Carol S. 2010. "Even Geniuses Work Hard." *Educational Leadership* 68 (1): 16–20.

Kelly, Betsy, Claire Hamasu, and Barbara Jones. 2012. "Applying Return on Investment (ROI) in Libraries." *Journal of Library Administration* 52, no. 8 (September–December): 656–71.

Kim, Bohyun. 2015. "Understanding Gamification." *Library Technology Reports: Expert Guides to Library Systems and Services* 51, no. 2 (February–March).

Locke, Edwin A., and Gary P. Latham. 2006. "New Directions in Goal-Setting Theory." *Current Directions in Psychological Science* 15, no. 5 (October): 265–68.

Pink, Daniel H. 2009. *Drive: The Surprising Truth About What Motivates Us*. New York: Riverhead Books.

Running in the Halls. 2011. "What's the Benefit to the Users." http://librarygame.tumblr.com/post/12145694181/whats-the-benefit-to-the-users.

———. 2015. "Lemontree: How Does It All Work?" https://library.hud.ac.uk/lemontree/about.php.

Snyder Broussard, Mary J. 2014. "Knowing When to Create a Library Game." In *Games in Libraries*, edited by Breanne A. Kirsch, 30–42. Jefferson, NC: McFarland & Company.

Wiggins, Grant P., and Jay McTighe. 2005. *Understanding by Design*. Alexandria, VA: Association for Supervision and Curriculum Development.

Designing Your Project

I F YOU HAVE EVER DESIGNED a game or a project that incorporates game-based elements, you already know that it can be difficult. Like an engine, a game includes many moving parts. Depending on the scope of your project and how immersive you want it to be, you might consider storyline, player avatars, levels, length, and format, all in addition to the content that makes the activity worthwhile for your patrons and relevant to your library. Even if your project or activity is not technically a game but includes gamification elements, familiarity with what makes games work can help you stave off headaches in the planning process and beyond.

It is worth noting at the outset, however, that game design can be complicated. Therefore, the ideas presented in this chapter will hopefully serve as a sampling rather than a *prix fixe* menu. As you sculpt your project, you should not feel as though you need to incorporate everything here. All that being said, attention to the structures and elements of games themselves can provide inspiration and ideas you can use as you work through the planning process. Designing games can be time-consuming, but attention to detail and player motivations can make it easier and can make your final product more effective. This chapter, then, will focus on game design as a way to create better user experiences, and hopefully by extension more patron enjoyment and use for your project.

⊚ Intrinsic vs. Extrinsic Motivation

At the outset, it is worth it to think about whether and why your potential players will want to play the game you are designing. People do things for different reasons, and these can include existing interest in a game or topic or a desire to get something—tangible or not—from the experience. Richard M. Ryan and Edward L. Deci describe two different types of motivation: *intrinsic* and *extrinsic* (2000). Put simply, intrinsic motivation includes what we do because we want to. Children's games are a good example of this type of motivation—children play because they like to and because they get enjoyment from it. Extrinsic motivation, on the other hand, comes from gaining a perceived benefit—good grades, rewards, etc.

The problem for libraries is that people behave differently depending on their type of motivation, and people who are only doing something because they expect a reward are likely to lose interest once that reward is removed from the table. More disheartening, there is an abundance of evidence to suggest that even people who start off with a real interest in a topic or activity lose interest once someone tries to motivate them through the use of rewards (Ryan and Deci 2000). In an interview with Ron Brandt, Alfie Kohn says,

> Rewards and punishments are both ways of manipulating behavior. They are two forms of doing things *to* students. And to that extent, all of the research that says it's counterproductive to say to students, "Do this or here is what I'm going to do to you," also applies to saying, "Do this and you'll get that" (Kohn 1995).

Even worse, manipulation of this kind can turn away people who may have started off with some level of interest in a topic or activity. "None of us enjoys having the very things we desire used as levers to control our behavior," Kohn says (1995). It is important to keep this in mind as you consider adding incentives or rewards to any type of game endeavor.

Because of the potential risks, you need to think carefully about the reasons behind each step of your game activity. Are you rewarding people for something they already find rewarding? While the use of rewards and incentives can have a place in the design of some game-related activities, they should be approached with caution.

⊚ Basic Elements of Game Design

Game design is the muscular heart at the core of your project: it provides the pulse that will drive your patrons' experience. Like a real heart, it will also need careful, customized attention and maintenance to stay healthy. It is also very complicated.

Game Design Tips

Hal Barwood (2001) describes game design as "an uncertain and murky endeavor." He does not seem to be alone in this assessment. Like many art forms, successful game design depends on psychology, design, story, visual aesthetics, and the general zeitgeist of a particular given moment. Being able to capture all of this and distill it successfully into game format is, at best, tricky. That being said, game designers have made attempts to decipher what makes a game successful. Hal Barwood and Noah Falstein, for example, worked for a time to collect what they called "The 400 Rules of Game Design"—pointers that would allow designers to identify best practices and understand what made them successful. Some of these rules are collected on Barwood's website, www.finitearts.com, but Barwood and Falstein acknowledge that 400 is something of an arbitrary number. There may be fewer rules, or (as is perhaps more likely), far more, and the spreadsheet currently available on the website has just over 110. Since game design requires at least some understanding of psychology, design, and storytelling, the rules can go in a variety of different directions, and they address a wide range of topics related to game development. Included on the rules sheet are what are referred to as Imperative Statements, which detail the principles of the various rules. Some of the most directly applicable rules for library gamification efforts are

- Provide clear short-term goals.
- Make subgames.
- Emphasize exploration and discovery.
- Begin at the middle.
- Make the game fun for the player, not the designer or computer.
- Be consistent in feedback. (Barwood and Falstein 2006)

However, it may be helpful for you to peruse the entire list, which provides guidance and inspiration for the creation of many different types of game experiences.

Jane McGonigal, the writer and game designer who created *SuperBetter*, also provides guidelines for game design. *SuperBetter* details a plan for incorporating various game elements into everyday life, where they are aimed at improving different aspects of it. McGonigal was inspired to write her book after she used elements of gamification to recover after a bad concussion, and in the book she details ways in which readers can use techniques taken from games to recover faster, develop strong support networks, and accomplish their goals. Although McGonigal's book is geared specifically toward helping people improve themselves in ways they see fit, many of her principles have clear applications for use in game design. Specifically, she gives seven rules for creating a more game-oriented life:

1. Challenge yourself.
2. Collect and activate power-ups.
3. Find and battle the bad guys.
4. Seek out and complete quests.
5. Recruit your allies.
6. Adopt a secret identity.
7. Go for an epic win. (2015, 9)

The principles collected by Barwood and Falstein and McGonigal are relatively easy to incorporate into game design as you think about your project. You may include various stages for your project; for example, teaching basic library elements at the outset, and then expanding this to require players to apply the skills they have learned. In a video game for children in a public library, the early levels might ask them to advance by answering trivia questions about the library. Once these are established, they might be able to defeat common enemies by discovering information using the skills they have honed already.

Even if your library has no natural "bad guys"—and hopefully it doesn't!—it may be possible to encourage patrons to take on avatars or new identities they will use to keep everything running smoothly. Perhaps library volunteers could be encouraged to think of themselves as secret library superheroes whose powers gain in strength as they help to shelve books, assist patrons with research, or design craft projects that can be used in story times. Friendly competition such as a leaderboard posted in a break-room can also help to keep players engaged in the project and can encourage them to go the extra mile to accomplish more (although emphasis should be made that *friendly* competition, entered into freely, is the key here).

Depending on the scope of your project, you may need to invest more or less time in the development of a game. A game that gives patrons points for checking out books and then returning them on time probably doesn't need a lot of analytical design planning in order to be a success. Patrons check out books and they get points, and they return them and get points—it's simple. But an involved game that incorporates elements of video game design (for instance, characters, fully developed worlds, and complicated motivations) will involve a good deal of investment, and may take months of careful planning to get right.

Types of Games

Not all types of games are appropriate for all circumstances. If your goal is to encourage young patrons to work together on a tree planting outreach activity for Earth Day that focuses on the idea that we are all connected, you will want to ensure that they don't see their efforts as a venue for competition with other teams. In this activity, all the patrons are working together to plant more trees and beautify the library grounds in order to make it a nicer space for the community. A game that emphasizes competition in this scenario may destroy the collaborative intention of the project and may not accurately reflect the hidden message, which is that taking care of spaces and nurturing more trees benefits us all. Competition in this instance could also serve to indirectly encourage patrons to sabotage each other's efforts by hoarding water, say, or attempting to make other teams' spaces less hospitable. In short, the type of game that you design tells the players about how you see the activity. It is important to make sure that your overall goal for the game doesn't get lost behind mixed messages.

Jose P. Zagal, Jochen Rick, and Idris Hsi (2006) identify three basic categories of games: competitive, cooperative, and collaborative. In competitive games, players work against each other to accomplish their goals—think of chess, for example, where a windfall for one player means a catastrophe for the other. In cooperative games, players work together in certain instances to effect good results for all parties. This may involve creating an alliance that momentarily helps both teams but is not set in stone. When the alliance becomes less beneficial, one of the teams may default. In collaborative games, players all compete together as one team that wins or loses depending on their efforts. They may need to make tough decisions for the good of the group that aren't always best for individuals. Collaborative games require players to think critically about their priorities and work together to nurture them. In the tree-planting scenario, for instance, one group may need to cede the planting area they have staked out as the best one in favor of giving the other groups better conditions too. What is slightly detrimental for one group ends up being to the benefit of all of the participants because now more of the planted trees are likely to thrive and grow.

In his book *Gamify Your Classroom: A Field Guide to Game-Based Learning*, Matthew Farber discusses incorporating the game Darfur Is Dying (MTVU 2015) into his world history class. Darfur Is Dying is a free, flash-based game that positions players as displaced people fighting for survival in a refugee camp. It was explicitly designed to provide a window into this experience to its players. Farber explains that in using the game with his class, he emphasized the ways in which it reflects the real experience of the people it is about.

> The game's tension provided a compelling experience for my students. They are in the flow channel, focused on getting water without getting caught. The lesson concludes with an exit ticket asking, "Why do you think this game was so hard to play?" Here, students can make the connection about struggling as a refugee in Darfur, because the mechanics are perfectly aligned with the message. (2014, 58)

Farber was able to use the game, in short, to lend credence to his class lesson, and the game's difficult structure reinforced this aim, ensuring that students understood the message.

You will want to carefully consider how your goals for your project dovetail with these various game categories. Questions to ask include

- What are the goals of the project?
- What category best meets these goals—a friendly competition, a collaboration, or an experience with cooperative elements?
- Does what patrons are doing reflect these project goals?

Consideration of these categories will help you design and develop a game that keeps your goals and your patrons' goals firmly in mind.

Video Games

Much has been written about video game design and the complicated structures present in many video games. James Paul Gee identifies thirteen principles he believes should be present in good computer or video games, noting that "the stronger any game is on more of the features on the list, the better its score for learning" (2004, 17–19). These principles are listed below, along with added brief summary statements.

1. Co-design (Players need to feel like they are part of the game, changing it by their participation.)
2. Customize (Players need to be able to make decisions in the game that affect its structure and what they learn.)
3. Identity (Players must feel a connection to the character they are controlling or creating.)
4. Manipulation (Players may feel like they have more control over actions they are able to take at a distance—for example, turning on lights in a room across town.)
5. Well-ordered problems (Early problems players face should help them learn how to solve problems they encounter later.)
6. Pleasantly frustrating (Players should feel they are able to complete the various tasks being asked of them, even if they are difficult.)
7. Cycles of expertise (Players should hone skills until they achieve mastery and then learn to adapt them to other scenarios that make things more difficult. Think of a peloton of bikers cruising through a suburban neighborhood and then suddenly relocating to San Francisco, where they need to contend with hills, traffic, and congestion in addition to the basic skills needed to ride in formation.)

8. Information "on demand" and "just in time" (Players should get help when they need it, and right when it is most useful.)
9. Fish tanks (These are less-complicated worlds that can emphasize important aspects of a game.)
10. Sandboxes (These are safe places in which to learn new skills.)
11. Skills as strategies (Learning should be a way for players to achieve something they want to achieve.)
12. System-thinking (This is the context for what players are learning.)
13. Meaning as action image (Players should gain insight through direct experience.)

There are ways to incorporate Gee's principles even in relatively simple games. In a scavenger hunt–style game created to teach college students how to use the library, for example, an early challenge incorporating the principle of well-ordering problems could ask the students to find the call number for a particular book. A later challenge might ask them to travel to the book's physical location. A challenge after that might require that they survey other books on the shelves and identify themes they notice in the Library of Congress cataloging system, thus connecting the book's location with the ins and outs of library organization.

In a self-guided tour of the library that patrons complete for points toward raffle tickets, it may be possible to include various tour options that are different lengths and geared toward different patron library-ability levels. For example, there may be one tour designed for self-identified library novices, and another that includes insider information and advanced searching techniques designed for library experts. This will help patrons customize the experience they are having with the tour and allow them to make decisions that shape what they will see and learn.

Video games have long worked to appeal not only to players' interests, but also to their emotions. Since they are generally totally voluntary, these games need to work from a basic understanding of their players in order to draw them in and hold their attention. This marks a contrast with many educationally focused video games in that the creation of an experience is the top priority rather than the attainment of quick skills and memorization. While games that focus on learning material quickly can help students study, they will probably not become go-to activities for very many people. In 2009, game developer David Perry and writer Rusel DeMaria published *David Perry on Game Design: A Brainstorming Toolbox*, which spends over one thousand pages detailing various aspects of video games, including sections on storytelling, characters, and designing player experience, while partially explaining some of the appeal and technique of video games. The extensive detail in the book and focus on so many aspects of design speaks to the level of complexity involved in creating a good game. While most library gamification activities and projects will not need to approach production at this level of detail, there is much to be learned from video games about what it takes to create something that really appeals to users.

Perry and DeMaria identify the establishment of goals as essential to holding player interest. They name three different categories of goals: long-term, intermediate, and moment-to-moment.

[The goals] form a hierarchy of the player's experience and direction in the game. At the top of the hierarchy are the long-term goals, which provide the overall framework for the player's experience. Below that in the hierarchy are the intermediate goals. You might think of them as short-term goals, but that could be misleading. Intermediate goals are of variable length and are started and (hopefully) completed during the course of pursuing the game's long-term goals. . . . Moment-to-moment goals are based on decisions the player makes, which in turn are based on immediate feedback from the game. (2009, 569)

In a library video game that asks players to solve puzzles on a quest designed to help them understand Boolean operators, for example, a long-term goal might be to complete the game (and therefore understand Boolean operators), while an intermediate goal might be to move up to the next level. A moment-to-moment goal might involve dodging bad guys who are insistent that players use *or* to connect the concepts *lion taming* and *cooking*.

Even if you are not thinking of creating a video game or video activity in the context of your library, video games still can provide fruitful inspiration. For example, if you are creating an activity where patrons will move through the library in teams, you might want to think about structuring their experience so that it mirrors a journey. While most library games don't set up alternate personalities or avatars for their players, you may want to think about whether this could work in your setting. It is possible that high school students in an instruction session, for example, might be more willing to experiment with library databases and resources if they feel like they are just controlling characters in the context of a game rather than making themselves vulnerable by looking through holdings and potentially coming across information they don't understand.

The rich worlds of some video games may also serve as an inspiration—particularly if you are thinking of creating a themed night or detailed group activity in your library. In a library orientation scavenger hunt, for example, teams could create themed names, and library staff could use costumes or props to immerse participants in the setting. Although something on this scale this may be difficult to organize (and would require significant buy-in from library staff!), done right, it could serve both to draw students into the library and to show them by extension that the library cares enough about their learning to try to create interesting experiences for them.

Board Games

Compared to video games, board games can seem deceptively simple. Many library patrons (and library staff members) probably remember quiet afternoons spent playing games like checkers, Monopoly, Chutes and Ladders, and Sorry! as children. These games, and many other childhood staples, rely largely on luck: what space a player lands on, whether or not a property already belongs to someone, or how closely other players are following can make all the difference between winning and losing. In Chutes and Ladders, for instance, player progression depends entirely on the number rolled during their turn and whether this number corresponds to forward progress or a trip down a chute. A player's roll decides whether the outcome will be a quick win or a protracted loss. Still, there is much that can be learned from board games, even if the game experience you are planning will not be in this format.

Board games can be fairly complicated, which allows them to draw in players more effectively. For example, the cooperative board game Eldritch Horror, from Fantasy Flight Games, includes multiple card decks, dice, counters, and other pieces. Game play includes opportunities for players to trade with each other, change locations, and perform what are referred to as Special Actions, which are unique to particular characters (Mastrangeli 2014). Players are able to make many different choices for themselves, and these choices allow them a lot more latitude than they might have in a simpler, scaled-down game.

Similarly, Pandemic, also a cooperative board game, designed by Matt Leacock, enlists players to fight against various viruses in order to save the world from deadly diseases. Each player takes on a particular role and can move around the board, treat diseases, and collect cards to help them heal people. Much of the board is taken up by a map of the world, which makes it easy to get a bird's-eye view of the viruses as they spread through the population in various areas. Because the game is cooperative, players need to work together and help each other in order to finally win (Nichols 2013). Both Eldritch Horror and Pandemic offer their players choice and don't rely simply on the luck of the draw.

These games go beyond simple roll-and-move strategies to give their players a real stake in what is happening and to encourage them to work together. Players are able to carefully consider what they see in front of them and make educated guesses about what might be coming next. This format has a lot of promise for use in a library setting, especially in a classroom where students are working to support each other's learning. Although board games are often complex and detailed in terms of artwork, plotting, and social dynamics, it may be possible to use them as a source of inspiration, especially for an ambitious project.

One major strength of board games is that players are physically located in the same space as they play. This can open up communication and allow for different types of games—for example, games that are more collaborative or that give their players the option to work together. Although communication can happen in other sorts of games as well, there can be various barriers that make it more difficult. Communication can allow players to really experience the game as an interactive and social event and can make it simpler for them to enter into a flow state where they lose track of time and become totally immersed in the world of the game.

Additionally, board games (and other types of games) can provide what Brian Mayer and Christopher Harris (2010) refer to as "authenticity." Put simply, authenticity in this context means that players need to develop the skills necessary to succeed in the game in order to compete. This means that instead of asking players to develop skills for the purpose of later completing a quiz or assignment, board games can move this process forward more naturally. In Monopoly, for example, which in other ways relies partly on luck, players need to be able to add up their money in order to determine whether they have enough to buy a property. Though being able to add is not the point of Monopoly, it is a skill that players may hone and practice through playing the game. That being said, Mayer and Harris caution against using too many games that are designed with specific educational purposes in mind, noting that "too often they fail to engage students in an enjoyable game experience; just as with bad books, students see right through bad games. Instead we look for games that gamers play" (2010, 75). Mayer and Harris describe the game Amun-Re, which centers on auctions, as a game that was not specifically designed for educational purposes, but which contains opportunities for them anyway.

> By combining multiple types of both hidden and open auctions, Amun-Re forces middle-school students to consider their opponents in a different way. This very authentic game, however, also happens to provide a powerful introduction to ancient Egypt. While playing the game, students are using vocabulary and encountering ideas such as the separation of Old and New Kingdoms and the importance of the river Nile. (2010, 75)

Amun-Re, then, speaks to the power that games can have beyond their ostensible goals, and it also highlights the fact that games used for educational or instructional purposes do not have to be dry and boring in order to provide benefits and skill-attainment for their players.

ⓖ Audience Considerations

As you plan your game or project, it is a good idea to give careful thought to the makeup of your audience. Who are the people who will play your game? What types of activities might be appealing to them? What might be motivating? What types of activities might they not be interested in?

In the article "Orientations to Video Games among Gender and Age Groups," Bradley S. Greenberg et al. suggest that the answers to these questions may be more difficult to ascertain than it might seem at first. Although their findings—which center on video games—indicate that men and boys spend far more time engaged in gameplay and seem more highly motivated to do so, the authors point out that video games have historically been created by men for an assumed male audience. "Rather than arguing that females are less competitive or even less interested in video games," they write, "the present findings (and those likely to be found in commercial market research efforts) will remind the industry to design games that better fit the preferences of young females" (Greenberg et al. 2010, 254). This has ramifications for library-designed game efforts as well and may serve as an enticement to think beyond the types of games available on the mass market when deciding how to structure your project.

It is important not to stereotype your audience. If you make false assumptions about what they might enjoy based on their age range, gender, or culture, you run the risk of alienating them or losing their interest—think of a little girl who loves baseball but whose only game options have to do with princesses and unicorns instead of sports. On the other hand, activities that give no consideration to these (and other) characteristics may also send your potential patrons running in the other direction. (Imagine that same little girl presented with a game designed for law students.) If it is at all possible, you should make an attempt to ask patrons ahead of time what types of activities they enjoy. This can take the form of small focus groups, polls, or informal questions posed to patrons you know well. If you work in an academic or school library, you might be able to arrange this fairly easily by asking student workers or visiting classes to try your game and give you feedback before you launch it. In a public library, you might ask library volunteers or frequent patrons for their thoughts. Small tokens of gratitude can help enormously—candy or a slice of pizza may be enticement enough for many patrons to want to help. Asking ahead of time may help you avoid designing a project or game that no one is interested in being a part of.

The following questions may help to provide a fuller picture of your potential audience.

- What is your audience's age range? In a mixed audience (e.g., children of different ages and their parents) you will want to find ways to appeal to all audience members. *Sesame Street* on PBS has long put this into practice, featuring segments that appeal to preschoolers alongside adult celebrities and jokes about media and world events.
- Are there particular books, television shows, themes, etc., that you can be reasonably sure all your audience members are familiar with? This may apply to a class of children visiting the library after spending time studying a unit on history, or

to senior citizens who will be doing research about an event they read about in a book club.

- Does your audience share common cultural touchstones? An audience comprised of people who share a common language or background would fall into this category, as would an audience made up of people who share particular challenges or interests. Examples of audiences who might share a common culture include people from particular neighborhoods, ethnic backgrounds, or language groups, in addition to people who live with disabilities or people who spend a large amount of their time studying a particular topic. Designing activities for individuals who are part of a common affinity group may allow you to include more specific, structured elements tailored directly for them.
- Does your audience have any pressing concerns or common worries? This may include high school seniors thinking about what to do after they graduate, or parents who are interested in finding out more about activities available for children in your area.

Thinking about your audience's needs and wants will help you create an activity that will be more appealing to them. The following sections will present the results of research into what types of activities are especially suitable for various groups. You will want to take all of this with a grain of salt, however. After all, you know your audience and your community best, and you can learn even more by talking to them and getting to know them better.

Player Types

In "Hearts, Clubs, Diamonds, Spades: Players Who Suit MUDs," Richard A. Bartle (1996) identifies four main types of game players, distinguishable by their playing style:

- achievers
- explorers
- socializers
- killers

According to Bartle, players who fit these types have corresponding gameplay characteristics. Achievers are motivated by getting points and advancing; explorers enjoy learning new things and discovering hidden aspects of the game system; socializers enjoy spending time with other players and see the game as secondary; and killers enjoy what Bartle calls "imposing themselves on others," whether this happens via killing other players' avatars or by disrupting someone else's game.

It would be a mistake to assume that the way a person plays a game is directly related to how they live their life. Some people may be simply experimenting with various aspects of their personality—seeing how they fit in the context of the game (Farber 2014).

What is more, a game that is designed with just one of these player types in mind may be frustrating or irritating to players who do not fit within that type. In an interview with Matthew Farber, Bartle points out that games that only appeal to one player type will ultimately alienate people who want to play in different ways, diminishing the game's effectiveness. Not all of your players will want to spend their energy trying to earn a high number of points. If you include elements that appeal to other player types, you have a better chance of engaging more of your overall audience. In the University of Huddersfield's Lemontree game, for example, players are encouraged to use library services to get points—but they are also able to socialize, compare their progress, and discuss the game with each other (Running in the Halls, 2015). This allows Lemontree to appeal to both Bartle's achiever and socializer player types, and it encourages wider participation. Incorporating elements that appeal to as many player types as possible into your game will enhance its success.

It also should be noted that depending on the activity you have planned, player types will be more or less important. Bartle himself, in the interview with Matthew Farber, discusses how player types might not align with gamification efforts in general. "They look at my Player Types Model because they know it works for games," he notes, but the people designing gamification projects are "not writing games. What they really want is a screwdriver, but no one's invented a screwdriver yet, so they use my hammer, which I suppose is better than trying to turn it with their teeth" (Farber 2014, 135).

Valerie Walkerdine (2004) adds more nuance to this consideration of player types in her exploration of ways that players might manage gender roles as they play. Reporting on the results of a detailed case study that focused on watching small groups of girls play video games together, she explores various ways that players used the game as a way to negotiate power and their identification with aspects of femininity. Although the players she observed overtly positioned themselves in roles such as winner, killer, loser, etc., their analyzed interactions suggested far more subtle negotiations than might be outwardly apparent. Players of a game, like any audience, are influenced heavily by the constructs and rules of their society, and while over-attention to this probably won't help your design plan, it may be instructive to keep in the back of your mind.

While gamification is by definition using elements of games in order to create more successful experiences and activities for patrons, not every element of gamification will be applicable to your project. You will want to think like a game character and always be on the lookout for ways to apply the skills you already have to the task you have at hand.

Age Ranges

Your library may serve patrons who are different ages. While age does not necessarily determine how someone will feel about an activity, it is important to think about it, especially in terms of your project's complexity and themes. One nice thing about incorporating game elements into library services is that many of these elements are easily adaptable. For example, the Kahoot! learning platform (https://play.google.com/store/apps/details?id=no.mobitroll.kahoot.android&hl=en) allows teachers to customize content to create game show–style activities in their classrooms. This gives them the chance to test students on their knowledge and have them informally compete as they put it to use. While it may not be a perfect fit for most library services, Kahoot! and other similar games can be adapted to meet the needs of students both at various grade levels and in various classes.

If you are planning an activity that will appeal to people of all ages, it may be helpful to include elements of personalization. For example, young children may be encouraged to visit every information station at an interactive event whereas older children may compete in activities for prizes. There are many ways to allow player personalization, including offering different tracks for completion. In a game where participants obtain points for completing a self-guided tour, for example, some players may choose to explore a particular aspect of your library in great detail, while others may try to visit all relevant spaces. Allowing players to choose what track they will complete grants them autonomy and gives them multiple avenues for success, which may translate to better participation.

It will also be helpful to think about ways to value your patrons' skills and experience. Games in a school library, for example, can build on the social skills students are already developing in their classes and at home, whereas games designed for senior citizens who enjoy using the library might find ways to reward them for the knowledge they have accrued throughout their lives. One way to do this might be asking seniors questions about events and experiences they remember, or asking them to work in teams that include young people. In this way, each group member can contribute their own skills and expertise, and the team set-up encourages players to think about the value each person brings to the table. If at all possible, honoring and celebrating the experiences that your patrons bring to your activity will help both to encourage them to participate and to allow them to build on prior learning in order to succeed.

⊚ Designing the Library Stars Tour

The Library Stars Tour was designed explicitly with its patrons' needs in mind. It directly reflects the absence of library instruction available to students in first-semester introductory writing classes at its university, and it attempts to engage professors by providing a service that may be beneficial to both students and faculty alike. Some student needs and characteristics taken into consideration by the game include

- Students are enrolled in introductory writing courses where library research will prove to be beneficial to their studies.
- For the most part, students have not spent a great deal of time in the library, and they may be unfamiliar with academic libraries in general.
- Students are new to the university (if not to college as a whole) and may or may not know much about the culture of the town where it is located.
- Since students are relatively new, they may not know very much about entertainment venues that are available or about who on campus can help them if they need support.
- Students will need to be able to conduct library research for other classes as they progress with their studies.
- Professors may value the resources and tools the library has to offer but may not know how to fit library instruction into their schedule for each class.

Since one of the game's goals is to engage students and help them to overcome their library anxiety, many aspects of the game have been designed with an eye toward increasing student comfort. Some of these aspects include

- Students can choose to work alone or in groups.
- The game is structured around a relatively silly, local theme.
- The game's premise reflects the community surrounding the university.
- Players who finish the game can win prizes, which helps to encourage motivation.

At the same time, the game's structure reflects the values of the library: although the game is casual and silly, it also includes valuable information and encourages students to make connections with library staff. The welcoming atmosphere that the library hopes to create for students taking the tour will hopefully encourage them to return over and over as they work their way through college.

Lastly, the very structure of the game reflects messages the library wants to impart to its newest patrons. Students at the university in the first few weeks of the semester often spend a lot of time sitting passively and absorbing information from faculty and other campus partners, and this can be draining day after day. The action-oriented tour flow, whereby students walk through the library and explore, helps to get them moving and allows them to see for themselves what the library has to offer.

Overall, the design of the Library Stars Tour aims to connect with students at the library's home college by teaching them about available resources, providing them with an engaging means of exploring the library, and pointing out valuable resources in the town or city of the university, such as movie theaters and restaurants. Since the game is geared toward new students, making them feel at home and fully supported at the university is an important step toward both student and library success.

ⓖ Key Points

This chapter has explored various points to consider as you think about the design of your game or activity. Although you may pick and choose between the ideas presented here (there is no need to use them all at the same time!), a basic understanding of game design and what goes into the creation of a successful game will help you to consider your project from different angles. Game design is a creative art in many ways, and as such, there are few hard and fast rules that apply in every situation. Consideration of audience, goals, and the type of experience you are hoping to provide for patrons is essential. Keep in mind these points:

- Game design is tricky. Good game design often allows players room to explore and grants them space for different types of success.
- When designing your game, you need to think about intrinsic versus extrinsic motivation—players who are already motivated to learn will lose interest if you try to push them toward learning with extrinsic rewards.
- Games should be

  ○ challenging, but not so challenging that players give up
  ○ a way for players to experiment with different aspects of their identity
  ○ planned around the needs of their players

- Games and game elements can help patrons enjoy their experience, but they can also serve to devalue services if not employed appropriately. You will want to think about the messages and ostensible goals of your game as you design it.
- Your audience will be the driver of your game design. It is essential to find ways to tailor your project to their needs, goals, and hopes—and to find ways to value their experiences and let them shine as the players of your game. A game that works for one audience may not work for another, and you will want to consider age ranges, cultures, and other factors as you work to plan your event.

In the next chapter, you will learn more about working with stakeholders both inside and outside the library and making a case for using gamification elements to support your core services.

References

Bartle, Richard A. 1996. "Hearts, Clubs, Diamonds, Spades: Players Who Suit MUDs." http://mud.co.uk/richard/hcds.htm.

Barwood, Hal. 2001. "Finite Arts." www.finitearts.com/Pages/speakerpage.html.

Barwood, Hal, and Noah Falstein. 2006. "The 400 Project Rule List." www.finitearts.com/pages/400page.html.

Farber, Matthew. 2014. *Gamify Your Classroom: A Field Guide to Game-Based Learning*. New York: Peter Lang.

Gee, James Paul. 2004. "Learning by Design: Games as Learning Machines." *Interactive Educational Multimedia* 8 (April): 15–23.

Greenberg, Bradley S. et al. 2010. "Orientations to Video Games among Gender and Age Groups." *Simulation & Gaming* 41 (2): 238–59.

Kohn, Alfie, quoted by Ron Brandt. 1995. "Punished by Rewards? A Conversation with Alfie Kohn." www.alfiekohn.org/article/punished-rewards-article/.

Mastrangeli, Tony. 2014. "Eldritch Horror Review." Board Game Quest. www.boardgamequest.com/eldritch-horror-board-game-review/.

Mayer, Brian, and Christopher Harris. 2010. *Libraries Got Game: Aligned Learning through Modern Board Games*. Chicago: American Library Association.

McGonigal, Jane. 2015. *Superbetter*. New York: Penguin.

MTVU. 2015. "Darfur is Dying—Play mtvU's Darfur Refugee Game for Change." www.darfurisdying.com/aboutgame.html.

Nichols, Tyler. 2013. "Pandemic Review." Board Game Quest. www.boardgamequest.com/pandemic-board-game-review/.

Perry, David, and Rusel DeMaria. 2009. *David Perry on Game Design: A Brainstorming Toolbox*. Boston: Charles River Media.

Running in the Halls. 2015. "Lemontree: How Does It All Work?" https://library.hud.ac.uk/lemontree/about.php.

Ryan, Richard M., and Edward L. Deci. 2000. "Intrinsic and Extrinsic Motivations: Classic Definitions and New Directions." *Contemporary Educational Psychology* 25:54–67.

Walkerdine, Valerie. 2004. "Remember Not to Die: Young Girls and Video Games." *Papers* 14 (2): 28–37.

Zagal, José P., Jochen Rick, and Idris Hsi. 2006. "Collaborative Games: Lessons Learned from Board Games." *Simulation & Gaming* 37 (1): 24–40.

CHAPTER 5

Identifying Partners and Making a Case

IN THIS CHAPTER

▷ How to identify potential project partners and stakeholders

▷ How to set common goals and objectives for your project

▷ Some ways you can make a case for gamification

▷ Some ways other librarians have developed successful collaborations

▷ Tips for successful collaboration and project management

EVERYONE NEEDS FRIENDS. It is likely that your project may benefit from the perspectives and expertise of people outside your department, or even outside the library altogether. Librarians of all stripes can find allies and partners as they plan activities, and these collaborations are often fruitful and valuable to all involved. That being said, as with any endeavor that involves people working together, there is also ample space for potential conflict. Thinking carefully about how to work with your partners and stakeholders as a team can go a long way toward smoothing communications and allowing your project to proceed effectively.

The 1939 children's book *The Country Bunny and the Little Gold Shoes*, written by DuBose Heyward and illustrated by Marjorie Hack, provides an idealized example of how these collaborations might work. Early in the book, a large family of rabbits finds success and industry by allowing each individual to take care of one task, from cooking to cleaning to providing entertainment by singing and painting pictures. One very small rabbit even contributes by pulling out his mother's chair for her when she sits down to eat. In this way, each family member helps provide for the rest, and no one bunny feels overworked or excluded. While your game-related partnerships may not end up being quite so idyllic, careful management and clear communication can go a long way toward the implementation of successful projects.

Partners and stakeholders are (1) the people you might work with outside your department or library as you design and implement your project, and (2) the people who have an interest in your project's success. Partners in a large-scale, scavenger hunt–type activity, for instance, might be nearby departments or businesses. In a public library, a neighboring sandwich shop might be interested in providing refreshments as a way to advertise their services. Depending on your library's setting, it might be possible to develop a scavenger hunt that ventures outside the library as well. School librarians might decide to design an activity that has students journey through both the library and the music room, for example, highlighting the benefits and services of both while at the same time allowing students to gain more familiarity with the school. Stakeholders for a public library service that provides homework-help resources for middle and high school students might be the students themselves who benefit from the resources, in addition to their parents and teachers.

Though the potential cast of partners and stakeholders for every project is vast, it is vitally important to give some thought to how to work to develop relationships with these interested parties. In "Influence without Authority: Making Fierce Allies," Kacy L. Allgood notes,

> No matter what you call it, libraries and librarians need allies that will support the library during times of prosperity or poverty. The goal is to create long-lasting relationships with library clients who recognize and publicize the value of library services. (2013, 30)

Consultation and collaboration with the people who have an interest in your project—no matter who they are—will help to ensure that the project is as helpful and relevant as it should be.

Partnerships

When you are considering possible partnerships, you might ask yourself these questions:

- Who else in the community has related or similar services?
- Who in the library might be interested in or affected by this game? (It is important to check in with other departments in your library, especially if your activity will have a direct impact on their spaces and services.)
- Is there a large event coming up in your community or school that will involve multiple departments or organizations?
- Could your library benefit from working with an organization that has similar goals or complementary services?
- Does another department or organization already provide a service you would like to work with them to expand?

Examples of possible potential partners are students, nearby or related organizations, teachers, other departments, and library staff.

In an academic library, for instance, you might look to collaborate with the writing program on campus to develop a game that teaches students about information literacy. By working together, you may develop a richer student experience that meets the goals of both areas. In a public library, you might try connecting with local organizations to meet shared goals. Vigo County Public Library in Terre Haute, Indiana, for instance, worked with various nonprofit groups in their area to develop websites for the nonprofits after the library determined that it was difficult to find information about many of these organizations. The websites helped the nonprofit groups by providing them with a Web presence, and they also helped the library because they provided both connections to the groups and accurate, available information that could be shared with interested patrons. Jeanne Holba Puacz, writing about this project, says that "what started as a simple idea for making information about local nonprofit organizations more accessible has now developed into a profitable partnership between the library, the local nonprofits, and the community" (2005, 15).

Stakeholders

You might begin to identify possible stakeholders by asking these questions:

- Who (besides the library) might benefit from this project?
- Who inside the library might benefit or experience challenges as a result of this project?
- Who might be affected by this project's outcomes?
- Who might be affected by the project's implementation?
- Where will the money for this project come from?

Stakeholders might be students, families with young children, neighbors, library staff, potential donors who want to help implement the game, area schools whose students may get a boost in reading, etc.

Stakeholders will play a key role in your project's success or failure. Although there are similarities and areas of overlap, stakeholders differ from potential partners in that they will not necessarily work with you to develop the project (although certainly in some cases they may). They may simply be people who have an interest in it one way or another or who stand to feel its impact. The key word here is *people*. In *Fundamentals of Project Management: Project Stakeholder Management*, the authors emphasize that stakeholder views and decisions are impossible to predict entirely accurately and may be influenced by forces and events outside your control. Careful consideration of stakeholder concerns and wishes is important as you design and implement your project (Eskerod and Jepsen 2013).

Partners and Stakeholders in the Longer Term

Most partnerships and collaborations are relatively short-term, lasting only as long as a particular project (Eskerod and Jepsen 2013). That being said, this does not mean that the bridge between various organizations needs to be gated shut at the close of an activity. It is possible that previous collaborations may be helpful in the future, or that successes might encourage more projects. Above all, these alliances are relationships that need to be sustained and nurtured, even quietly, after the main part of an activity is over.

Partners and stakeholders, especially in collaborations that are meant to benefit the interests of multiple departments or parties, can truly hold life-or-death importance to the success of a project. Eskerod and Jepsen make this clear:

We repeatedly read about projects that apparently "went wrong"; some failed to generate the stipulated benefits, others were never finished and petered out along the way, while still others were afterwards not seen as successful even though they were carried out as planned. A recurring theme in these failures is project managers who have not taken sufficiently into account the interests and motivations of the persons and entities that can affect or be affected by the project, the so-called *project stakeholders*. (2013, 1)

An important part of the planning process for your game or activity will therefore necessarily include consideration of who these people might be and what their involvement in the process might look like. You might begin to think about ways to keep your activity or project going for longer than you might have initially anticipated, or you might decide to develop new activities that will continue your collaboration. All of this will need to be clearly laid out in order to avoid confusion and miscommunication. You should ask partners questions about what they hope to gain from a project, and communicate your own goals as well. Stakeholders in various areas may have opinions and views that you haven't considered, so communication with them is essential. Once you have complementary goals, it may be useful to see how you can expand on them in future projects. Ultimately, no one will benefit from a relationship that is explicitly manipulative or dismissive, so you will want to make sure to approach your activity from a place that honors the wishes of all parties.

◎ Working with Collaborators to Establish Common Goals and Objectives

Setting library goals for your activity is discussed elsewhere in this book, but it is also worth thinking about how you will work with project partners and stakeholders to set goals that will help drive the project. Goals are essential. In their study of effective teams, Carl E. Larson and Frank M. J. LaFasto report,

> First, high performance teams have both a clear understanding of the goal to be achieved and a belief that the goal embodies a worthwhile or important result. Second, whenever an *ineffectively* functioning team was identified and described, the explanation for the team's ineffectiveness involved, in one sense or another, the goal. (1989, 27)

Put shortly, in order to succeed in developing your game, you and your collaborators must identify and work toward a common, clearly articulated goal. And the library's goals will not be the only ones present as you plan. In a partnership between a library and a campus writing program, for example, both parties might share a goal to increase student information literacy, but the library may have an additional goal to bump up use of services, and the writing program may have its own goal of improving student writing. These goals are not mutually exclusive; if students use more library services, their writing and research skills may improve relatively organically, just as better student writing may include use of more library services. That being said, you will want to think about what common goals your share with your partners and stakeholders, and what complementary goals you can use to both encourage their participation and enrich the benefits your gaming activity will grant its players or participants. It is worth it to have a discussion with your collaborators about your library's goals for the project, their own goals, and the goals that you might share.

In "New Directions in Goal-Setting Theory," Edwin A. Locke and Gary P. Latham elaborate on the importance and implications of setting goals in a variety of contexts as a way to accomplish more and attain success. They find that the establishment of relatively difficult, specific goals "[leads] to a higher level of task performance than do easy goals or vague, abstract goals such as the exhortation to 'do one's best'" (2006, 265). The importance of goals in various contexts is difficult to overstate—goals will help you and your partners and stakeholders determine what is important, and ideally they will guide your project as it unfolds. Careful consideration and open communication will help as you work to determine which goals are the most important for your project.

Locke and Latham acknowledge that goals set by individuals may at times be in conflict with goals set by larger groups, writing that "having high personal goals that were compatible with the group's goal enhanced group performance, whereas having personal goals that were incompatible with the group's goal had a detrimental effect on how well the group performed" (2006, 266). This underscores the importance of working closely with team members in an open and transparent manner to ensure that everyone is on the same page and that the interests of one group do not cast a shadow over those of another.

Beginning the Conversation

A possible script for beginning the conversation that will help determine whether you and your collaborators are in agreement might look something like this (yours will of course depend on your situation and activity and may need to be tailored toward your partners):

> I'm really excited to be working on this project with you! The library is hoping that this game will help increase student information literacy and will also drive traffic to our databases and services. I want to make sure that we can work together to meet the needs of both of our departments—what are you hoping to see as a result of the project?

Where you go from there will vary, depending on the personalities involved, history, and context, but it may help to establish up front what you are hoping to gain and then give your partners and stakeholders the chance to discuss what their own hopes and desires are as well.

One way you might begin to recognize the needs of your partners while at the same time keeping track of your own is to decide up front which collaborator will take responsibility for which aspects of the project. When Broward County Library and Broward County Community College in Florida decided to build a shared facility, for example, they decided to task the community college with construction and furniture orders, with the county library being responsible for hiring and training new staff (Passalacqua 1999). Though both parties shared the costs associated with the new facility, this plan allowed each to take ownership of a particular aspect of the project and helped to minimize potential for conflict.

Questions you might ask as you begin to discuss the project with partners and stakeholders include

- What is the overall goal for the game?
- What is each collaborator's or area's goal for the game?
- Who will be responsible for what game aspects?
- What resources will you need and how will you get them?
- What information or deliverables do you need from each collaborator?
- What does each collaborator need in order to accomplish their goal?

- How much time will the development of the game take? What deadlines can you set to ensure that everything is finished on time?
- How will you hold yourself and other project members accountable?

Answering these questions ahead of time may help to facilitate the planning process and work to ensure that no one's toes are stepped on as you move forward.

Smooth Group Communication

Much has been written about effective communication and processes in group situations. Rather than rehash all of the ins and outs of working in groups, this section will focus instead on making sure that you and your partners can establish an understanding as you work together. Communication is key when you are working with your collaborators. It will allow you to specify clearly what you are hoping to accomplish with your project, and it will help you understand others' needs as well. In Shari Caudron's essay "And the Point Is?" she tells the story of a young man she once saw standing by the side of a road with a sign that read "Won't work. Not hungry. Need beer" (2000, 20). Caudron was inspired by this young man because, as she puts it,

> What passes for communication in organizations is really nothing more than vague references to desires, thoughts and ideas. We may think we're communicating with others, but in reality most of us are only hinting at what we want to accomplish. (2000, 20)

The young man, by contrast, was being remarkably direct about his needs and requirements. He had a much better chance of getting what he needed than, for instance, someone who only hinted at their interests or who tried to minimize them. At the same time, his clearly stated goals were also a bright signal to people who were uninterested in his approach and helped them stay away.

While it is important to communicate politely and professionally with all of your partners and collaborators, it is also important to let them know exactly what you need and what you think. It is equally important to find out this information about them. If you only leave hints, there is a much greater chance that your needs won't be met, and this can lead to hard feelings and missed opportunities. Similarly, asking good questions and clarifying group-member statements will help you come closer to understanding their needs. Working in a group provides the benefit of others' experiences and thoughts, but it is easy to miss this benefit if you or they are not as clear as you might be.

In their book *TeamWork: What Must Go Right/What Can Go Wrong*, Carl E. Larson and Frank M. J. LaFasto (1989) report the results of their research into what makes successful teams. According to them, effective teams have

- A clear, elevating goal
- A results-driven structure
- Competent team members
- Unified commitment
- A collaborative climate
- Standards of excellence
- External support and recognition
- Principled leadership

Aligning goals for your project with goals for individual areas and departments will help immensely in establishing buy-in and smoothing your collaboration process. As you work with partners and stakeholders, it is crucial to set standards and encourage each other to work toward results. Establishing how the members of your group will work together and ensuring that each individual is committed to the project's success will aid greatly in making your project effective and reflective of the needs of all relevant parties.

Active Listening

Having an open, collaborative project necessitates active listening, which requires that all parties make an effort to understand each other's perspectives and needs without talking over one another.

> When people are listened to sensitively, they tend to listen to themselves with more care and to make clear exactly what they are feeling and thinking. Group members tend to listen more to each other, to become less argumentative, more ready to incorporate other points of view. Because listening reduces the threat of having one's ideas criticized, the person is better able to see them for what they are and is more likely to feel that his contributions are worthwhile. (Rogers and Farson 1987, 1)

Of course, making sure that you are actively listening to someone is hard work! Rogers and Farson write that in order to listen actively, it is important not to give advice or try to change the person who is speaking—instead, the listener should try to understand what they call the *total meaning* behind the speaker's words and take notice of what the speaker may be sharing through tone, body language, or other indicators. They recommend an exercise during a spirited conversation that asks each contributor to stop and repeat the argument of their opponent to their opponent's satisfaction before moving on to their own point. This will allow both people to feel heard and can provide a richer understanding of argument nuance as the conversation progresses.

Similarly, Beebe and Masterson recommend that you take a "stop, look, and listen" approach before responding, namely by identifying and silencing distractions, observing gestures and other nonverbal cues, and asking yourself questions such as "How would I feel if I were in that person's position?" "Learning to quiet one's own thoughts and to avoid prejudging others is a first step," they note. "Fully understanding others . . . involves considerable effort" (2006, 142). They recommend that you ask questions to ensure that you understand what the person is saying and that you repeat back what they have said in your own words in order to make sure that you have a good handle on it.

While it is possible that your discussions with partners and stakeholders will be amicable and simple, it is still crucial to be able to listen to them effectively in order to assess whether you understand their viewpoints and needs. People don't always say exactly what they mean, especially at first, and active listening can help you avoid frustration and conflict by exposing the heart of an individual's concerns. A deeper discussion of the issues and opportunities inherent in your project will allow it to grow and develop into something that is richer than it might be with only one perspective included. This can also allow you to construct strong bridges with your collaborators, and it can potentially open doors for new projects in the future.

Managing Conflict

Any time people gather together, there is potential for conflict. Disagreements can stem from competing interests, opposing opinions, misunderstandings, and simple personal animosity. Some conflict is also productive: people who disagree and discuss their opinions may unearth deeper, more balanced understandings of issues, and they can work together toward constructive solutions that account for varying concerns and viewpoints. Still, in the case of arguments that threaten the productivity or even existence of your group, there are steps you can take to manage conflict and prevent it from derailing what you have worked so hard to accomplish.

First, it is important to understand that sometimes conflict cannot be satisfactorily resolved. In some cases, people hold intense convictions about particular viewpoints and will not accept compromises that they see as undermining them. While this can be frustrating, it is also an unfortunate fact of life, and there is no real way around it. Beebe and Masterson write,

> If you find yourself arbitrating a conflict in a small group, first decide which issues are most likely to be resolved. If you assume that all conflict can be resolved just by applying the right techniques, you may become frustrated. However, you must also be wary of the self-fulfilling prophecy. If you hastily reach the conclusion that the conflict cannot be resolved, you may behave in a way that fulfills your prediction. (2006, 171)

Beebe and Masterson provide some suggestions for dealing with various types of conflict, which center around listening to people, making sure their views are being expressed accurately, and attempting to prioritize issues that need to be resolved. Their suggestions for managing what they call "simple conflict," or "disagreement over a course of action idea, policy, or the like" (2006, 175), are listed in textbox 5.1.

Of course, these suggestions will not quickly resolve any and every potential source of disagreement. There may be situations where there is no real, acceptable solution or compromise, or situations where the individuals involved may not be willing to work toward an acceptable solution. More detailed books and other resources are available if you find yourself embroiled in such a volatile conflict.

TEXTBOX 5.1

SUGGESTIONS FOR MANAGING CONFLICT

1. Listen and clarify perceptions.
2. Make sure issues are clear to all group members.
3. Use a problem-solving approach to manage differences of opinion.
4. Keep discussion focused on the issues.
5. Use facts rather than opinions as evidence.
6. Look for alternatives or compromise positions.
7. Make the conflict a group concern rather than an individual concern.
8. Determine which conflicts are the most important to resolve.
9. If appropriate, postpone the decision while additional research is conducted. This delay also helps relieve tensions. (Beebe and Masterson 2006, 175)

⊚ Making a Case for Gamification

There are many benefits to developing games and game-inspired activities in your library, including the potential for enhanced learning, the chance for closer connections to patrons who are interested in games as a hobby, and the opportunity to drive traffic to services and areas. There is also potential to connect more fully with patrons of all ages and to provide them with better service and experience. Aaron J. Elkins writes that "by playing games, school librarians can share common experiences with some of their patrons, and use this shared experience to develop stronger relationships with them" (2015, 63). This potential benefit goes beyond school librarians. In "Reasons for Playing Casual Video Games and Perceived Benefits among Adults 18 to 80 Years Old," Susan Krauss Whitbourne, Stacy Ellenberg, and Kyoto Akimoto report that in their study, adults sixty years old and older actually played Bejeweled Blitz, the game they were examining, more frequently than younger adults (2013). While games played for fun differ from game-inspired activities or events in a library setting, the popularity of games across age groups means that they can be a good way to connect with a variety of different people. This also may mean that you don't need to confine game-related activities to the children's or young adult programming sections of the library.

More detail on how and why games can be so helpful can be found elsewhere in this book, but it is important to have a grasp of how this might work as you think about making your case for a game-inspired project or activity. Here is a brief (and by no means complete) primer on some of the reasons it may be beneficial to your library and your patrons to develop activities based on games.

- Games can help people learn. In many games, in order to move forward, a player has to figure out how to succeed within the context of the game. In order to do this, they need to learn (Gee 2005).
- Games can let people try on new identities (Gee 2005), which they can then use to make mistakes and experiment without major repercussions.
- Game play appeals to people at all ages, and some middle-age adults claim that games help them with stress relief, among other benefits (Whitbourne, Ellenberg, and Akimoto 2013).
- Social media has made electronic or online games almost ubiquitous, driving up use and popularity in many different groups (Johnson, Adams, and Cummins 2013).
- There is evidence that playing video games can result in improved cognitive function, although direct effects may be limited (Blumberg et al. 2013).
- Games help us solve problems and work through issues and ideas (Bettelheim 1987). Trying something out, whether it is developing study skills or learning the ins and outs of a database in a game, may make it easier to approach later when the stakes go up.

When you pitch your idea to partners, stakeholders, or contributors, you may want to consider mentioning some of these potential benefits in order to strengthen your case. Many people may not realize that games can have appeal for people in such a wide range of age groups. Several e-mail templates are provided in textbox 5.2 as suggestions or jumping-off points for you as you begin to think about making your case to possible partners or stakeholders. Of course, you will always want to make sure to fit any of these templates to your proposed activity, audience, library context, and goals as you see fit.

TEXTBOX 5.2

POSSIBLE E-MAIL TEMPLATES

For a Potential Partner or Contributor

Hello,

The library is working to develop an orientation for families who are new to the area. We are interested in developing a self-guided game that families can play together, based on research that shows that games can help facilitate learning and solve problems. We are hoping to make this fun and interactive in order to increase participation and engagement with the library and the community, and wondered, since your services tend to complement ours, if you might be interested in partnering with us. We'd love to meet to discuss this idea whenever you are free. Thank you for your consideration, and please let us know if you have any questions.

For a Potential Stakeholder

Hello,

The library plans to pilot a self-guided orientation game for new families this winter. We believe that this will help to increase our engagement with the community and can showcase our services and resources. Since you are a valued member of our community and our library, we were wondering if you might be able to provide feedback or input on our plan. We believe that it has a much better chance of success if it reflects the needs of real families who are new to the area. We'd like to invite you to a reception and meeting—heavy appetizers provided—where we will share more about our plan and ask for your ideas and input. Thank you for being such an important part of our library, and we hope to see you soon.

For a Library Colleague

Hello,

Access Services has been thinking recently about developing a new incentive system to encourage patrons to return checked-out items on time. In particular, we are thinking about creating a special drawing patrons can enter every time they return materials before the due date. Participation would be voluntary and based on rewarding people for returning materials rather than on singling them out for not being as punctual. We have been really impressed with how effective the library IT Department has been in terms of training student workers and providing service, and we were wondering if you might be interested in working with us to make this a reality. We value your insight and feedback, and we would love to schedule a time to talk about this in more detail.

When you think about pitching your idea to your partners and stakeholders, it is essential to keep in mind their priorities and concerns and to address these up front as much as possible. You will need to show them why your game or activity is important and how it will tie in to the overall goals of the library or campus. Good attention to others' thoughts and needs will go a long way toward making your potential game a reality.

◎ Examples of Collaborations between Libraries and Other Groups

Collaboration can be a beneficial way both to engage outside partners and to deepen and develop more innovative services. The examples below illustrate various types of collaborations between libraries and other areas, and they may serve as inspiration as you consider how to situate a game or game-like activity of your own. Because different libraries necessarily have different needs and different patron groups, the examples below are organized by type of library (academic, school, public). This doesn't mean, however, that similar collaborations couldn't be established, for example, by a public library using an academic library's idea as a template, or vice versa. These examples are merely meant to give you an idea of how you might engage with your particular patrons in order to provide the best service.

Academic Libraries and Student Groups

The following examples come from academic libraries where staff and librarians worked to capitalize on their built-in connections with student groups in order to provide better, more tailored services for their patrons.

University of Minnesota–Twin Cities Libraries

After some time spent experimenting with various game-based events, the University of Minnesota–Twin Cities Libraries realized the importance of basing these programs directly on collaboration. They have since worked with student groups in order to develop game-based activities that stem directly from student interest. One example involves a collaboration with Society for Physics students, with whom they partnered to provide demonstrations of Oculus Rift, a virtual-reality headset. Librarians also developed an exhibit based on technology for a local arts festival, and sponsored talks with student groups about aspects of the gaming industry. They found that their previous attempts at integrating game nights and events into their programming had not been as successful as they had hoped, and they emphasized the need to understand their particular community in order to work with its members (Bishoff, Farrell, and Neeser 2015).

Seeley G. Mudd Library at Lawrence University

While the Seeley G. Mudd Library has engaged in a number of partnerships with student groups and other stakeholders, one particular collaboration of interest is the one they had with a student club focused on the role-playing card game Magic: The Gathering. Initiated by a student, the event was able to help the club grow and help the library establish and deepen relationships with its patrons. Because Magic players tend to own their own cards, club recruitment efforts to reach casually interested, potential new players could be a challenge. The library and the club planned an event together, which included a "cube draft" of cards owned by the club. This allowed more players to participate, and it allowed the library to work collaboratively with the student organization. Because the event was hosted in the library, it also meant more student traffic and appreciation of library spaces and areas. Of additional interest is that the student who approached the library to begin with had been inspired by other game-events held there, which underscores the potential for collaborative efforts to grow and inspire new projects (Vanden Elzen and Roush 2013).

Academic Libraries and Campus Partners

Academic libraries are fortunate to have many potential campus partners who share their goal of providing good service to their students. The following are examples of some of these collaborations.

Z. Smith Reynolds Library at Wake Forest University Live-Action Gaming Events

The Z. Smith Reynolds Library at Wake Forest University has partnered with its school's Division of Campus Life and other collaborators to host Capture the Flag and Humans vs. Zombies events in the library. These events take place when the library is closed and involve students running through library spaces in teams to accomplish various game goals. Although these games do not introduce students to library services in a traditional manner, they do encourage students to see the library as a welcoming, fun place that exists for them. Writing about the events, Hubert David Womack, Susan Sharpless Smith, and Mary Beth Lock note that "the Z. Smith Reynolds Library has found that the 'Capture the Flag' and 'Humans vs. Zombies' big game events are exceedingly successful, low barrier ways to engage students in a nonthreatening, nonacademic way. These are models that offer some scalability for a wide variety of libraries" (2015, 214).

Muckrakers Game at Gelman Library at George Washington University

Librarians at Gelman Library designed the Muckrakers Massively Multiplayer Online Role-Playing Game (MMORPG) for incorporation into library instruction in an attempt to maximize student enjoyment and encourage students to learn together. In collaboration with the University Writing Program (UWP), librarians at George Washington typically teach a four-credit freshman course focused on "critical thinking, collaborative learning, and peer evaluation" (Brown, Ceccarini, and Eisenhower 2007, 227). Librarians decided to develop a game based on journalism that could be used with this course. The game asked students to pretend to be new reporters working in groups for liberal, conservative, and independent publications. Students would conduct research individually and then in groups, competing to be the writer of an upcoming feature story in their publication. The stories needed to focus on current events and political news, which tied in with course curriculum, and evaluation centered heavily on peer input. After developing and piloting the game, the library showed it to the faculty teaching the university writing course it corresponded to. Although they were unable to test the game with students due to budgetary and staffing difficulties, they received positive feedback in the form of supportive comments and ideas for further development from faculty (Brown, Ceccarini, and Eisenhower 2007, 231).

Public Libraries

Public Libraries have had success in partnering with various collaborators, including authors, patrons, and other libraries. The following examples illustrate some of the ways public librarians may work with stakeholders and partners to develop exciting new gaming activities.

Toronto Public Library's Keep Toronto Reading Program

Jim Munro, a science fiction writer and game designer, heard about the Toronto Public Library's 2013 Keep Toronto Reading selection *Fahrenheit 451* and was inspired to pitch an alternate reality game for the event. Interested participants called a number and listened to the voice of a book character, who assigned them missions. Missions included participants recording themselves reading passages from the book, and posting pictures to social media. The event was popular and attracted 120 phone calls on its first day. The culmination came in a live event open to anyone at the library (Schwartz 2013).

National Teen Library Lock-In

Public libraries often host events during National Teen Library Lock-In (https://sites. google.com/site/teenlibrarylockin/home), which encourages teens across the country to go to their public library, play games with other teens, and participate in contests and crafts. In 2014, eighty libraries participated. In 2015, some libraries incorporated the popular Minecraft video game in their offerings. The Minecraft incorporation worked well, and players enjoyed the chance to compete against each other and experiment in the world of the game (Haines and Makled 2014).

North Melbourne Library's Minecraft Gaming Day

Recognizing the importance of young patrons in their library, which is in the vicinity of a variety of schools, North Melbourne Library in Australia sought to work with these young people to create an event. "Challenging the traditional programming approach of designing *for* young people and creating a program *with* young people, this program drew on the knowledge and enthusiasm of the young North Melbourne community," writes Rachael Cilauro (2015, 88). The collaboration began with a group of six regular patrons, of various ages, who met weekly to discuss gaming with librarians. It culminated in a gaming day focused on Minecraft. The response to the event was positive, with both patrons and librarians mentioning how much they had enjoyed it. Overall, the event served to illustrate that young people can be great collaborators with strong ideas and insight you can use as you plan for the future.

School Libraries

School library partnerships may take the form of collaboration with specialists or groups, or they can include partnerships with other libraries, classroom teachers, or groups of students.

Encouraging Students to Design Games

Brian Mayer, a gaming and library technology specialist for the Genesee Valley Educational Partnership, wrote in *School Library Journal* about his collaborations with various school districts. Using as a template and model the Parsley Game system, which is "an interactive fiction model based on the old computer text adventures like *Zork*" (Mayer 2012), students in area schools develop game ideas and then figure out how to make them work. Then Mayer, the teacher, and the school librarian conference with each group of students to give feedback and suggestions. At the end, each group plays each other group's game and shares ideas about design and how well it has managed to reflect the curriculum the students are working on.

Writes Mayer, "This program has been incredibly rewarding . . . more importantly, [students] are engaged in a process that initiates inquiry, problem solving, team building, collaboration, cross-curricular connections, informative and procedural language, and content mastery" (2012, 23). By connecting individuals across the district, this project is able to reach a variety of different students and engage them more closely with the curriculum.

Stump the Librarian at Salome Ureña Middle Academies (in Partnership with the New York Public Library)

Students at the Salome Ureña Middle Academies in Manhattan were able to practice developing research questions and could attempt to stump New York public librarians in a collaboration between the school and the New York Public Library (NYPL). The collaboration stemmed from a unit at NYPL called the Connecting Libraries and Schools Project, and it involved students thinking of questions to ask visiting librarians while other students and school community members watched. The visiting librarians were able to use reference materials and school library materials to answer questions, and they had to be able to find the answer within ten minutes. Participating students received small prizes. The event was successful, both in terms of increasing traffic at the school library and area public libraries, and in terms of encouraging students to build connections with librarians. The public event met with the enthusiastic approval of both participants and onlookers (Schaffner 1995).

ⓖ Stakeholders and Collaboration in the Library Stars Tour

Asking questions early on can help to determine stakeholders and possible collaborators for the Library Stars Tour. For example,

- Who inside the library might be affected by this project?
- Are there stakeholders outside the library on campus or in the community?
- How do library goals for the game align with the goals of other stakeholders on campus?

As is often the case with games created by academic libraries, potential player interest does not exist in a vacuum. The goals of the library are intrinsically linked to the goals of other academic areas on campus—in this case, the writing program. The success of the Library Stars Tour will hinge largely on librarian relationships with writing program faculty who will ask their students to complete the tour. Because of this shared interest, librarians designing the game would benefit from including faculty members in the planning process. The game can better meet the needs of these stakeholders if they are given a voice. Other stakeholders on campus besides faculty members in the writing program include

- students
- library staff members and student assistants—especially those who will directly interact with students as they complete game activities
- faculty not necessarily involved in the introductory writing program
- computer lab staff or other staff who work in or near the library

Additionally, the Library Stars Tour presents the prospect of establishing and developing relationships off the university campus. Because of the tour's direct tie to the community where the university is located, there is a clear opportunity available to reach out to local businesses and individuals who may be interested in partnering with the project. Partnerships such as these can be mutually beneficial—for example, the tour indirectly advertises area movie theaters by providing prizes and coupons students can use, and the businesses are given the chance to reach out to and build stronger relationships with new residents. In turn, this may make students feel more comfortable in their new community, and it may help them transition more smoothly into college life. Questions you may work to answer with partners and collaborators include

- Who will be in charge of what?
- What is the timeline for the game? When does each piece need to be ready?
- What are the goals for each area or department? How can these be met?
- What is the overall purpose of the game and how can it be best accomplished?

Clear, courteous communication with all stakeholders will be essential in this process—the library will need to work with collaborators to determine how best to meet the needs of all interested parties, and there may be disagreements along the way. That being said, the inclusion of multiple voices should overall serve to enrich player experience and help to nurture partnerships that may last longer than the timespan of the game.

ⓖ Key Points

This chapter focused on how to identify and work with potential project partners and stakeholders as you plan your game-based activity or event. Partners and stakeholders can add immensely to the richness of your project and can be chief determinants of its level of success. Fostering close, respectful collaborations will allow you to fully develop your current project and can open the door in the future to additional game-based, and other, partnerships.

- Think broadly about potential partners and stakeholders. Depending on the circumstances of your library and the specifics of your game, you may consider asking for the opinions of

  - Students
  - Other departments
  - Frequent patrons
  - Neighbors
  - Other libraries
  - Library staff and volunteers

- People make partnerships—use active listening skills and respectful communication to honor your collaborators' needs and to plan your game together.
- Although it is impossible to avoid all conflict—and inadvisable anyway!—there are steps you can take to ensure that your game project does not become so mired in individual differences that it is unable to move forward.
- Make a case for your game by focusing on how it can meet larger library, community, or school-related goals.
- Take inspiration from other libraries that have forged partnerships and collaborations with outside individuals and groups.

In the next chapter, you will read about various types of game-related projects that have been carried out at other libraries.

ⓖ References

Allgood, Kacy L. 2013. "Influence without Authority: Making Fierce Allies." In *The Machiavellian Librarian*, edited by Melissa K. Aho and Erika Bennet, 29–47. Burlington, VT: Elsevier Science.

Beebe, Steven A., and John T. Masterson. 2006. *Communicating in Small Groups: Principles and Practices*. 8th ed. Boston: Pearson Education.

Bettelheim, Bruno. 1987. "The Importance of Play." *Atlantic* 259 (3): 35–46.

Bishoff, Carolyn, Shannon L. Farrell, and Amy E. Neeser. 2015. "Outreach, Collaboration, Collegiality: Evolving Approaches to Library Video Game Services." *Journal of Library Innovation* 6 (1): 92–109.

Blumberg, Fran C., Elizabeth A. Altschuler, Debby E. Almonte, and Maxwell I. Mileaf. 2013. "The Impact of Recreational Video Game Play on Children's and Adolescents' Cognition." *New Directions for Child & Adolescent Development* 139 (Spring): 41–50.

Brown, Ann, Paola Ceccarini, and Cathy Eisenhower. 2007. "Muckrakers: Engaging Students in the Research Process through an Online Game." In *Sailing into the Future: Charting Our Destiny—Proceedings of the Thirteenth National Conference of the Association of College and Research Libraries*, edited by Hugh A. Thompson, 226–36. Chicago: American Library Association.

Caudron, Shari. 2000. "And the Point Is?" *Workforce* 79, no. 4 (April): 20.

Cilauro, Rachael. 2015. "Community Building through a Public Library Minecraft Gaming Day." *Australian Library Journal* 64 (2): 1–7.

Elkins, Aaron J. 2015. "Let's Play!" *Knowledge Quest* 43, no. 5 (May/June): 58–63.

Eskerod, Pernille, and Anna Lund Jepsen. 2013. *Project Stakeholder Management*. Burlington, VT: Gower Publishing.

Gee, James Paul. 2005. "Learning by Design: Good Video Games as Learning Machines." *E-Learning and Digital Media* 2, no. 1 (March): 5–16.

Haines, Claudia, and Jack Makled. 2014. "National Library Lock-In Event Features Authors, Games, and Minecraft." *School Library Journal SLJTeen eNewsletter*. www.slj.com/2014/08/programs/national-library-lock-in-event-features-authors-games-and-minecraft/.

Heyward, DuBose, and Marjorie Hack. 1939. *The Country Bunny and the Little Gold Shoes: As Told to Jenifer*. New York: Houghton Mifflin.

Johnson, Larry, Samantha Adams, and Michele Cummins. 2013. *NMC Horizon Report: 2013 Higher Education Edition*. Austin, TX: New Media Consortium.

Larson, Carl E., and Frank M. J. LaFasto. 1989. *TeamWork: What Must Go Right/What Can Go Wrong*. Newbury Park, CA: Sage Publications.

Locke, Edwin A., and Gary P. Latham. 2006. "New Directions in Goal-Setting Theory." *Current Directions in Psychological Science* 15, no. 5 (October): 265–68.

Mayer, Brian. 2012. "Get Kids Designing: Student-Created Games Combine Curricular Concepts and 21st-Century Skills." *School Library Journal*. www.slj.com/2012/08/opinion/the-gaming-life/get-kids-designing-with-student-created-games-the-gaming-life/#_.

Passalacqua, Debbie. 1999. "Broward Community College." In *The Librarian's Guide to Partnerships*, edited by Sherry Lynch, 5–12. Fort Atkinson, WI: Highsmith Press.

Puacz, Jeanne Holba. 2005. "Libraries + Nonprofits Add Up to Profitable Community Partnerships. *Computers in Libraries* 25, no. 2 (February): 13–15.

Rogers, Carl Ransom, and Richard Evans Farson. 1987. Excerpt from *Active Listening*. In *Communication in Business Today*, edited by R. G. Newman, M. A. Danzinger, and M. Cohen, 1–5. Lexington, MA: D.C. Heath and Company.

Schaffner, Judith. 1995. "Yo! I Stumped the Librarian!" *School Library Journal* 41 (August): 42.

Schwartz, Meredith. 2013. "Toronto Public Library Enters Alternate Reality (Gaming)." *Library Journal*. http://lj.libraryjournal.com/2013/04/marketing/toronto-public-library-enters-alternate-reality-gaming/.

Vanden Elzen, Angela M., and Jacob Roush. 2013. "Brawling in the Library: Gaming Programs for Impactful Outreach and Instruction at an Academic Library." *Library Trends* 61, no. 4 (Spring): 802–13.

Whitbourne, Susan Krauss, Stacy Ellenberg, and Kyoko Akimoto. 2013. "Reasons for Playing Casual Video Games and Perceived Benefits among Adults 18 to 80 Years Old." *CyberPsychology, Behavior & Social Networking* 16, no. 12 (December): 892–97.

Womack, Hubert David, Susan Sharpless Smith, and Mary Beth Lock. 2015. "Large-Scale, Live-Action Gaming Events in Academic Libraries." *College & Research Libraries News* 76, no. 4 (April): 210–14.

CHAPTER 6

Types of Games

IN THIS CHAPTER

▷ Questions to ask yourself as you determine what type of game will work best in your library

▷ Some ways libraries have incorporated games into their services

▷ Advantages and disadvantages of using various types of games

▷ What library services might be a good fit for games

ONCE YOU DECIDE that you want to incorporate games into your library's services, it can be hard to know where to start. Because of this, you may take inspiration from other libraries that have worked to develop games and game-related activities in the past. This chapter's focus is on sharing game ideas and projects from various types of libraries in the hope that you will be able to find or adapt an idea that will work in your setting.

There are probably as many successful game ideas as there are libraries, and this chapter will only skim the surface. In particular, the games profiled here are those that take the form of orientations; large-scale, one-off projects; training games; and games that are embedded specifically in the context of schools. By no means should this be taken to suggest that these are the only types of potential games available—there are many other ideas and categories, and these games represent just a sampling of what is out there. Depending on your library's needs and goals, you may decide to work to develop your own take on something that has already been done, or to develop a project that is entirely new.

Games can take many forms, from points-based library websites to large-scale, one-time-only events, and the success of your particular project will hinge largely on your library's context, patrons, and situation within your community, school, or other area. Before you begin to plan your game, you will need to think carefully about your goals for the project and how it will fit within your services. For example, if your game is based on patron understanding of a particular television show, book, or movie, it may not be sustainable as an annual event (depending on the popularity of the medium it is based on). Events that only take place one time can be fun and can be wonderful experiences for patrons, but they can also entail a lot of planning for a relatively short event. At any rate, it is a good idea to think carefully and critically about the game you are beginning to devise before diving too deeply into the planning process.

Questions You Should Ask as You Think about Your Game

Before beginning a project as potentially complicated and collaborative as a game, you will want to ask yourself questions to determine how best to go about the planning process. Though these are covered in more detail in other sections of this book, they are summarized here for your convenience. Specifically, you will want to ask yourself questions in the following areas.

Partners and Stakeholders

- Who *in the library* might be affected by or interested in this game? (Remember to think about people who may be affected by the game's presence in the library and impact on other services in addition to potential players. Depending on where and when the game takes place, there may be other people whose schedules are impacted.)
- Who *outside the library* might be affected by or interested in this game?
- Will you collaborate with any of these parties? Why or why not?
- If you collaborate, who will be responsible for what? How will you decide how to divvy up responsibilities?
- Will this game need additional funding? If so, where will it come from?

Setting Goals

- What *library* goals should this game fulfill? What *patron* goals should this game fulfill? How will you know these goals have been met?
- Does your project reflect patron interests or make the library or patron experience better in some way?
- Are your goals attainable?
- How will your game's design reflect your goals?

Audience

- Who is your target audience for this game? How will you plan the game so it appeals to them?
- What do you want this particular audience to be able to do or know as a result of having participated in your game?
- What interests and needs do the members of your projected audience have? How will the game reflect these interests and needs?
- What will you need to learn about your audience in order to effectively plan the game?

Game Design

- What kind of game are you creating? Will it be a relatively small activity or a large, immersive experience?
- How will your game's design encourage players to want to play the game?
- How will the game's format reflect your goals and intentions?
- What game aspects will you incorporate to enhance player experiences?
- What is your projected timeline for the game's planning, execution, and conclusion?
- How will you make the game fun for your players?

Answering these questions will not (unfortunately) tell you everything you will need to know as you begin to plan your game. However, it will help you begin to understand your audience, your goals, and how best to design your project so it speaks to both. Thoughtful planning in the earliest stages of your game's development will eventually lead to more successful outcomes and a more targeted game experience for your patrons.

Types of Games

There are many different types of games, from sports to board games to video games. It will be up to you to decide what type of game will work the best, both in the context of your library and in terms of framing the objectives you hope to attain. For example, a game designed to teach patrons how to use the online catalog probably won't involve a lot of long-distance running. The two activities don't seem to have many parallels you could draw on to situate the skills involved. That being said, a points-based video game that rewards players for completing objectives as they move through the online catalog may help both to teach and to actively encourage patrons to hone their research skills. There are certainly advantages and disadvantages to using different types of games, and it may help to know ahead of time what some of these are.

Defining Games

The *American Heritage Dictionary of the English Language* (2015) provides several definitions of the word *game*. Most salient to the purposes of gamification are these:

> 1. An activity providing entertainment or amusement; a pastime: party games; word games.
> 2.a. A competitive activity or sport in which players contend with each other according to a set of rules: the game of basketball; the game of gin rummy. . . .
> 6. (*Informal*) An active interest or pursuit, especially one involving competitive engagement or adherence to rules.

Games, then, are wide ranging. Not every game will be relevant to every situation. There are particular types of games that seem to be relatively easily adapted to fit within the auspices of library gamification. The following is not an exhaustive list, and for every rule there is an exception, but it may be instructive to get a feel for what types of activities have worked for other libraries in the past. These types of games can include

- Role-playing/simulation games
- Video games
- Board games
- Digital badges
- Scavenger hunt–style games and other team-based games

The game type you choose should complement what you want patrons to take away from your game. While any type of game will have advantages and disadvantages (some of which can't be avoided), it is a good idea to make sure that your game's structure aligns with your goals and hopes. In the article "What Computer Games Taught Me About Urban Planning," Daniel Hertz describes how the often-subtle interplay between a game's assumptions and its messages looks in two city-related video games, SimCity and Cities: Skylines. Hertz writes,

> Unlike when I was 10, I can [now] also appreciate that CS [Cities: Skylines], like Sim-City, has a whole host of assumptions about how cities work, and how urban governance works, built into the gameplay—assumptions that are both frustrating as a player and fascinating as someone who spends a lot of time thinking about real urban planning and governance. While all games that simulate real life are of course drastically simplified, the way that they're simplified often speaks to the actual worldview of the people who design and play them. (2016)

Elsewhere in the article, Hertz discusses zoning regulations, priority for traffic, and the absence of local politics—all of which are part of the games that must be taken for granted by players, and all of which may skew players' perceptions of the importance of these same things in real life.

None of this means that planning a game is impossible, however. To the contrary, many librarians and library staff members have worked with their colleagues to produce games that are meaningful, interesting, and instructional. Below are some descriptions of different types of games, with information about their various strengths and challenges. This list of games and game types is by no means exhaustive—your creativity can be your guide as you think about what direction you might go. That being said, these games may help to fire up your imagination as you imagine what a game might look like in the context of your own library.

Role-Playing Games

A role-playing game may encourage students to develop empathy for people who lived during different time periods or who faced challenges that those living today can't imagine. In *Minds On Fire*, Mark Carnes delves into the Reacting to the Past (https://reacting.barnard.edu/) games in use at many universities and colleges. Reacting to the Past games assign students roles in various historical events and ask them to act out these roles, basing their decisions and perspectives on primary documents. Students Carnes interviewed frequently underscored that their participation in the games helped them develop a better understanding of those with differing viewpoints—which in turn helped them develop an empathy toward others they may not have otherwise felt much for at all. Carnes writes,

> Perhaps a few years from now . . . we will all benefit from the time [these students] spent pacing in their dorm rooms, pondering antique moral dilemmas and imagining what it was like to walk in the shoes of people whose bones have long since turned to dust. (2014, 227)

Smaller-scale games can work this way as well, including in a library setting. In "Reenacting the Titanic: A Simulation Game Teaches Lifelong Lessons," Holly Cannon and Susan M. Blackman describe their work to develop a game for eighth graders that taught students about class systems while capitalizing on interest in the Titanic. Students were asked to confront moral dilemmas such as whether to let others get on lifeboats ahead of them, and they were required to adhere to rules that privileged certain students over others. Cannon and Blackman write, "The results were astounding. Not only did every student have only positive things to say about the activity, but each one also truly understood the basic unfairness of the class system" (2000, 76).

Although these games can be time-consuming to set up, and although there is an element of risk involved (will the players go along with the game? Will they participate fully?), satisfying games can provide long-lasting benefits for their participants. Examples of role-playing games are listed below.

Live-Action Role-Playing at Helen Hall Library

Helen Hall Library Teen Librarian Jenny Brewer developed a live-action role-playing (LARP) activity for patrons between eleven and eighteen years old. This activity was selected because it had "elements of plot and story, making it a good tie-in to reading in general" (Ries-Taggart 2010, 7). Over the course of seven weeks, participating patrons met to discuss characters and plot, gain points and privileges within the game, and work to develop their own backstories and motivations. Everything culminated in a banquet that celebrated the fact that the activity had "the highest and most sustained level of attendance the library has seen at any teen summer program in the last four years" (2010, 8).

Library Adventure Game at Appalachian State University

Faced with the challenge of providing training to staff and student workers, Belk Library E-learning Librarian Scott Rice and Instructional Materials Center Coordinator Margaret Gregor collaborated to develop a game to teach reference-service skills. The end result was a simulation game where players moved through various adventures online that asked them to answer reference questions typical of those they might face at the reference desk. Players chose between different answer options and received a grade after the conclusion of each interaction (Rice and Gregor 2010, 22).

Interested in whether or not the game was effective at teaching staff reference-service skills, Rice and Gregor assessed it by providing pre- and post-tests to participants. "After playing the game," they reported, "80–90 percent of respondents taking the post-test would choose the best response" (2010, 22). Part of the success of the game may have hinged on its ability to reflect the needs of various library staff members—questions included were similar to those that were routinely received at the desk in the school's Instructional Materials Center.

Zombies in Curriculum at Harrison College

After spending a few uninspiring quarters teaching a required two-credit information literacy course at Harrison College in Lafayette, Indiana, librarians Dawn Stahura and Erin Milanese wanted to try something different. Having identified two major problems in the structure and implementation of the course—student apathy, and poor student topic selection—Stahura and Milanese decided to incorporate a zombie theme in an effort to engage students more fully. While not strictly a role-playing game, what they developed did include aspects of role-playing as they asked students to envision an alternate reality taking place during a zombie apocalypse and then to write papers reflecting the reality they faced in these parameters. They did this by structuring the course around the premise that "a zombie apocalypse had occurred, leaving the world in utter chaos and destruction" (Stahura and Milanese 2013, 355). Research was presented as reports students would submit to the president of the United States in order to help ensure humanity's survival. Students selected topics for research such as "'disaster planning and preparation,' 'economic recovery after a disaster,' and 'mob-mentality and crowd control'" (2013, 355).

Stahura and Milanese report that the zombie theme was a success, resulting in stronger research papers and more student investment in course work. Though some students were initially confused about the topic or did not want to do research that pertained to zombies, Stahura and Milanese were able to clarify the basic points and assign non–zombie-related research to students who were not interested.

Video Games

Video games can be completed alone or in teams, and patrons can benefit from these games' interactive nature and structure that encourages skill mastery. Libraries can benefit from the fact that video games are hugely popular and appeal to people across age groups. The Entertainment Software Association (ESA) reports that 155 million Americans play video games and that 42 percent of Americans report playing video games three or more hours per week. Although many people associate video games with children and teenagers, the ESA says that the average gamer is thirty-five years old (Entertainment Software Association 2015). This means that video game activities can be developed to appeal to adults as well as young people.

M. Brandon Robbins, exploring the possibility of gaming events for adults in library settings, writes, "Offering adults-only gaming programs will only make your patrons more diverse, more trusting, and more enthusiastic" (2015, 51). Video game events come with a built-in cachet you can use to appeal to various patron constituents.

In addition to this, the fundamentals of video games offer insight into how they can be effective at reaching patrons and teaching them important facts about your library. "Good games call on players to navigate by trial and error, experimentation, and subsequent analysis of cause and effect," writes Liz Danforth. "No one gets it right the first time" (2011, 67). There is a powerful message here about learning and the search process, both inside and outside the library.

Designing and building a successful, interesting, and useful video game can be daunting, and it will definitely require effective collaboration between your library and people outside your library (at least if no one on your staff has experience with video game design). Video games are perhaps best thought of as an art form, and their creation can be challenging. After all, you most likely wouldn't decide to write a bestselling novel as a way to reach your patrons. However, if you can design a video game that patrons will enjoy and want to play, you will have a platform that allows you to reach them and build long-lasting, effective connections. Library video game examples are listed below.

Adventures in Research Game at the University of West Georgia

Librarians at the University of West Georgia worked to develop a video game that could function as a sort of online textbook for students enrolled in an online literacy course (Sullivan and Critten 2014). The game they developed was structured like a Choose Your Own Adventure book in that the players were faced with choices and then saw the ramifications of those choices play out during the game. Since the librarians had a particular look and style in mind, they hired a freelance artist to create the visuals and worked steadily alongside the artist to make sure that the segments reflected their vision.

The game met with positive feedback, and many students indicated that they preferred it to a typical textbook. Since the game was designed to adapt to campus needs, the creators continue to work to evaluate it and make changes as time goes on, basing their decisions on evaluations, testing, and other suggestions.

Information Literacy Instruction Video Games at Carnegie Mellon University

Librarians at Carnegie Mellon University took advantage of the school's Entertainment Technology Center (ETC), which allows students to work on projects designed to teach them about digital entertainment and to help them develop video games that will promote information literacy. Working alongside students in the program, the librarians developed ideas and collaborated to create games that would teach students about library concepts and structure.

Their final product, which was designed to have an old-school, arcade-game feel, centered around a fictional student named Max who needed to learn about information literacy concepts in order to improve his grade. When the game was tested with students, their reaction was largely positive. The students indicated that they enjoyed playing and would play the game again (Beck et al. 2008).

Board Games

Board games generally require players to sit together in one space, and they can involve collaboration, critical thinking skills, and strategy. Over the last few years, libraries and schools have begun to experiment by moving board games out of the box of leisure-time activities and into the curriculum. This has a lot to do with recent board games that involve more skill and thought than simple childhood games like Connect Four! and Candyland. Ticket to Ride (www.daysofwonder.com/tickettoride/en/usa/), for example, requires players to chart train courses across various maps, considering various strategies and thinking critically about how to manage time, resources, and space along the way.

In their book *Libraries Got Game: Aligned Learning through Modern Board Games*, Brian Mayer and Christopher Harris (2009) identify various ways that board games can help students grow and develop, specifically in school libraries. They emphasize that games can be a venue for skill acquisition, helping students to engage and think about problems from new angles. In addition, they underscore the social aspect of board games.

> With an increasing number of today's social interactions taking place online, students are at risk of losing the interactive experiences needed to build the face-to-face skills that are still relevant for their future success. This is why, when selecting gaming resources, schools should focus on gaming experiences that bring students together and foster social interaction. (2009, 27)

Players need to be in close proximity to each other, and this can help foster friendships and personal connections. This means, in part, that board games in libraries can encourage patrons to get to know each other better and to feel more at home in the library's community.

Interestingly, Mayer and Harris also connect board games to inquiry, noting that gameplayers' tendency to repeat games they enjoy in a familiar environment may encourage students to think about problems from new angles and try new strategies. "Through repeated exposure," Mayer and Harris write, "students learn to safely stumble, dust themselves off, and continue onward, perhaps on a new path or with a new goal in mind" (2009, 30). As the authors also say, "New board games involve a sophisticated thought process that challenges kids to think critically" (2009, 24). This type of learning can easily find a home in many school curriculums, and can serve as enrichment to students at other libraries as well. Below, you will find examples of ways board games have been used by libraries.

Defense of Hidgeon at the University of Michigan

Defense of Hidgeon is an online board game designed to be played by teams of undergraduate students. Developed to help students learn about how to navigate library collections, the game provides instruction in searching databases, print books, and other sources. Students enrolled in an Introduction to Information Studies course at the University of Michigan were recruited via incentives to play and share their thoughts with the game's developers (Markey et al. 2008).

The game's backstory centers on the Black Death, and the players' main task is "scrutinizing information in Duchy libraries about plagues, past, present, and future, in order to help the Duchy's ruler develop a plan of action. Students must prove they are the Duchy's richest, fastest, and most efficient team of researchers" (Markey et al. 2008).

Although the game was online, it retained the feel of a physical board game (the board set-up included thirty-four spaces players moved through, and players moved by rolling a digital die), and the student players reported working together in one room to improve their progress. Overall student reaction was positive, although some objected to tasks that required them to find information by physically going to the library. Reflecting on student responses that asked for a game that more closely incorporated work completed for classes, the Defense of Hidgeon team eventually moved on to create another game, BiblioBouts, that took these concerns into consideration (Smale 2011). Overall, Defense of Hidgeon represents a novel way of connecting students to the library.

The "Grab a Book" Game

Writing in *Teaching Pre K–8*, Carol Otis Hurst describes a board game that is accessible to children at many different grade and reading levels. The game board is designed to look like a house with a staircase running through it that players traverse as they progress through the game from the cellar to the attic. Hurst suggests that book titles be written at either end of the staircase, using a book title that mentions an attic or high space at one end, for example, and a book title that refers in some way to basements or low areas at the other end (1996). Gameplay is determined by dice rolls that move players up the staircase, and at particular junctures, players are directed to pick Grab a Book cards that feature questions about books they have read. The Grab a Book cards can be created by the game facilitator, and Hurst includes suggestions for questions such as "Which book family would you like to join for a week?" and "If you could only bring one book on a spaceship, which book that you have already read would you choose?" (1996, 85). The game's easy customization and adaptability means that it can be used with very young patrons in addition to school-age children either as a way to complement reading programs or as a fun activity that helps spark patron conversations about reading.

Digital Badges

At first glance, digital badges may not seem as game-oriented as some of the other activities in this chapter. Digital badges operate as a way of applying game elements, such as points and visible incentives, to real life. Put simply, digital badges are a way to reward people for attaining various skill sets and completing different tasks in various areas without enrolling them in formal classes or introducing them to other settings where this may traditionally happen. For example, a library patron who always returns his or her books on time might receive a badge to display online or in social media that celebrates this. Similarly, a student in a school library who demonstrates that he or she can use the catalog effectively might be rewarded.

Emily Rutherford, Katharina Freund, Heather Jenks, and Inger Mewburn write that "badges seem a natural fit for libraries, as they allow clients to receive official recognition for their engagement in library programs and training without the attendant coursework apparatus" (2015). Because libraries often function as a sort of "third place" where people congregate outside of home and work, it can be difficult to reward patrons and community members for taking part in activities there. Digital badges provide a game-inspired method for doing this.

Some libraries have integrated the sentiment behind digital badges into their websites, providing points for completing tasks and attempting to gamify the experience of using the library. While not every patron will find these types of draws to be convincing, some may see them as an encouragement to stretch their library muscles and reach out to use services.

Badges can be difficult to design, and some patrons may not be interested in learning more about them. Rutherford, Freund, Jenks, and Mewburn report that some people question whether badges are "serious" enough for people to work toward achieving. Despite this, adding digital badges to your library can help motivate some patrons to use services and resources, and they can also help in terms of establishing good, strong connections with users.

Digital Badges for Subject Librarians at Washington University in St. Louis

Drawing on the need for subject liaisons to understand research tools and skills involved in data management planning and geographic information systems (GIS), data and GIS librarians at Washington University in St. Louis developed a program that awarded digital badges to participants. Participation was voluntary, and sessions took place over the course of four afternoons. Completion of a capstone marked the culminating point of the entire experience, and digital badges that recognized the accomplishment were awarded to people who completed each track.

At the end of the program, librarians had awarded nine badges to colleagues who completed the sessions and capstone. Though evaluations of the program were generally positive, with a large degree of interest and enthusiasm expressed for the topics, 45 percent of the participants surveyed indicated that obtaining a badge had not been an incentive, and 33 percent of the participants indicated that they had not known about the badges. At the conclusion, organizers of the program were still deciding whether or not to continue using badges as a part of the sessions in the future (Hudson-Vitale and Moore 2016).

Worlds of Learning at New Milford High School

Laura Fleming, a school library media specialist at New Milford High School in New Jersey has developed a site, Worlds of Learning (www.worlds-of-learning-nmhs.com/), to help teachers at the school learn new skills and obtain recognition through digital badges. Badges awarded celebrate skills such as using Twitter, incorporating Google Classroom features into teaching, and using Padlet. The process of badge attainment is fairly simple: teachers register to use the site, select a tool to learn, learn about it, and then incorporate it into their instruction in order to earn a badge. The site is designed to encourage teachers to add various technological tools to their instruction repertoire, noting that "as technology integration continues to increase in our society, it is paramount that teachers possess the skills and behaviors of digital age professionals" (Fleming 2016).

Scavenger Hunts

A scavenger hunt, or game where patrons collect bits of information as they move through various spaces, may be an ideal choice if you want to encourage people to work together and get to know each other during the course of your game. Many libraries have offered scavenger hunts as a way to orient new students or patrons, capitalizing on the activity of the hunts (patrons moving through the library) in addition to the capability of scavenger hunts to encourage people to work together. Another benefit of scavenger hunts is their accommodation of large groups of people. Because there may or may not be a formal presentation included, it is less essential to secure a large room or to limit the number of participants.

Scavenger hunts have faced a certain amount of controversy, with some libraries attempting to limit their use by professors and teachers who send large groups of students unannounced to the library, armed with questions. There is some evidence to suggest that students may enjoy scavenger hunts more than other activities and that the hunts may help to reduce library anxiety (McCain 2007). In addition, libraries are often the points of origin for scavenger hunts incorporated into orientation activities, and these library-designed games seem to be met with less disapproval. Examples of scavenger hunts appear below.

Ghost Hunters at Pace University Libraries

Pace University librarians worked to develop a scavenger hunt that could be assigned to students in a seminar course for incoming freshmen. Jennifer Rosenstein writes, "The library used to provide in-person tours and orientations . . . however, this has become impossible, as the size of the freshman class continues to grow" (2013, 350.) To meet the need for library information for new students, she created a scavenger hunt based in the school's history "to introduce students to the library's physical layout, services, and online resources" (350). Centered around historical figures whose deaths had taken place near the campus, the game was intended to be included as a part of a freshman seminar course, University 101 (UNV 101). The rules of play asked students to travel through the library, gathering clues at disparate stations. Clues were of varying degrees of difficulty.

The game was available to players for six weeks, and promotion consisted of e-mail flyers and reminders sent to UNV 101 faculty. The hunt was generally a success, with mainly positive feedback, and most students reported they enjoyed the experience. In the future, the librarians plan both to change the game structure so that it is more of a traditional scavenger hunt and to find ways to make it more of a social experience (Rosenstein 2013).

Lafayette College Library Research Games

Lafayette College Library has experimented with several different orientation plans and activities. Because a library orientation for new students is not required, they have faced challenges in terms of encouraging student participation. In the fall semester of 2014, they decided to combat this issue by designing a Research Games activity based on the release of the second *Hunger Games* movie (Bailin 2015). The movie tie-in served as a draw for student participation and allowed the library to create other incentives, such as theme shirts with a movie-inspired tagline and "districts" that reflected language from the movie to encourage interest.

Students moved in teams through the library, returning library materials they had received at the start to their appropriate locations, where they learned about library services. Every few minutes, the teams rotated to learn about other locations. Although the event was not billed as a scavenger hunt, the players encountered many scavenger-hunt features, such as moving through different spaces and finding information that would help them complete their goals. Although an event like this has a limited lifespan (once students are no longer interested in *Hunger Games* movies, it will be more difficult to incorporate this game into services), it can be a fun way to encourage students to come in and learn more about the library. After gathering feedback to evaluate the Research Games sessions, librarians at Lafayette College Library decided to offer a series of tours in the future incorporating some of what they learned about appealing to students from the earlier sessions (Bailin 2015).

Ohio State University Libraries Game-Based Orientation

Following up on extensive research and design, the Ohio State University Library Instruction Office, together with the Office of First Year Experience and Office of Undergraduate Studies, developed a detailed, game-based approach to acquaint students with library services and spaces before they arrived on campus. Head Hunt: The Game was a central feature of this plan and required students to participate in a virtual scavenger hunt in order to find the location of a stolen mascot head (O'Hanlon, Diaz, and Roecker 2009). Incorporating features of both scavenger hunts and board games, the game involved an online campus map that showed various campus locations. In each location, students had the option to play games or watch videos or other supplemental materials. In one area, for example, a film showed current students discussing how the library had helped them. Games included crossword puzzles and multiple-choice questions, among others. Clues were awarded for accomplishing some game goals.

Overall, the game encouraged student engagement with the library and didn't penalize them for not knowing everything. In their article about the game, O'Hanlon, Diaz, and Roecker report that the game's areas of focus reflected what incoming students would most likely need to know right away as they came into the library, without going into exhaustive detail about more specialized collections or services. "Is this everything a student needs to know about the library? No, but this information will serve entering freshmen well, and is a richer (and more memorable) learning experience than a brochure pocketed into a very full orientation packet" (2009, 108).

Other Game Types and Game Examples

Not every type of game is included in the list of examples above. Because games are so varied and can go in so many directions, it is not possible to put them all into neat categories. Don't feel limited by games that have been designed only for libraries like yours. Your school library, for example, may find the kernel of an idea tucked away in a library orientation originally designed for an academic library and be able to use it to create something that reflects your own patrons' needs and space.

The games listed below may help you think about possible game projects in your library, and they could potentially be sources of great inspiration as you consider your library context, your patrons, and the goals you have for your services. It is ultimately up to you (armed, as you are, with the answers to the questions you've worked through above) to decide what to plan, whom to include, and how to get the word out in your own community. Examples of games that did not fit into any of the earlier categories are listed below.

Library Survivor at Corporate Landing Middle School, Virginia Beach

Library media specialists at Corporate Landing Middle School developed a game called Library Survivor (www.vaasl.org/pdfs/Conference_Handouts/2010/Schweers_Survivor-HandoutVema.pdf) to teach students about library services and offerings. The game is loosely based on the popular *Survivor* television series (www.cbs.com/shows/survivor/), which centers on teams of contestants sent to a remote location and forced to work together to survive and compete. Aligned to Common Core standards, the activity involves splitting students into teams, assigning roles to individuals, and then asking everyone to participate in challenges covering areas of interest, namely, "Boolean operators, databases, Destiny catalog, dictionary, Internet safety, media evaluation, thesaurus, website comparison, and website evaluation" (Flegal and Schweers 2014, 18). These could be modified in other library settings. Flegal and Schweers write, "We have been playing Library Survivor for a number of years now. We stress that it's all about information—how to find and evaluate it. Both teachers and students look forward to it each year" (2014, 18).

Technology Challenge at Brigham Young University

Upon realizing that the technological savvy of librarians at Harold B. Lee Library of Brigham Young University did not match that of students, library administration at the school sought to develop an incentive-based training program that would encourage librarians and staff to hone their skills. The program was self-directed, and it involved asking participants to commit to spending fifteen minutes per day learning a technology-related skill. After participants had spent one thousand minutes learning, they were awarded a bookstore gift certificate (Quinney, Smith, and Galbraith 2010). Progress was recorded online.

The project was a success, with "eighty-nine percent of the participants [reporting] that their desire to learn new technology had increased, and sixty-nine percent [reporting] that they are now able to learn new technology faster after completing the Technology Challenge" (Quinney, Smith, and Galbraith 2010, 209). Largely, this may have been due to the personal and self-directed nature of the project; participants could fit it in whenever they had a free moment and were able to choose what technology they were interested in learning. Because the entire activity was structured as a game with built-in incentives, it may have appealed to people who would not otherwise be as interested in technology (2010).

Nerf Capture the Flag at Carnegie-Stout Public Library

After closing time one evening per month, the Carnegie-Stout Public Library in Dubuque, Iowa, fills with blaster-toting patrons. Nerf Capture the Flag has proved to be a popular activity—one that often attracts people (predominantly men) in their late twenties and early thirties who aren't necessarily frequent visitors. In addition, the game helps to build community (Fuerste-Henry and Smith 2015). Participants—who must be at least eighteen—are required to bring their own Nerf blasters (though the library maintains a few backups), and the game is played in an area with evenly arranged shelves and a mezzanine that players use for air power. The library has worked to develop and refine its rules—among them, requiring that players don't modify their blasters and that people make an attempt at being good sports.

Overall the events have been a success for the library. Andrew Fuerste-Henry and Sarah F. Smith write, "Everyone has fun, staff included, and the sheer novelty of it has drawn attention from around the community . . . it's well worth the slight nuisance of a reference section full of foam darts" (Fuerste-Henry and Smith 2015, 23).

A-Maze-ing After-Hours Harry Potter Party at Denver Public Library

Amy Seto Forrester, a children's librarian at the Denver Public Library, worked with colleagues to design and build a giant cardboard maze in an open hall and then invited children and their caregivers to a special after-hours Harry Potter–themed event to celebrate it. During the event, participants played Harry Potter–inspired games, had the opportunity to view the maze from higher floors in the library, and ventured into the maze itself, which included more Harry Potter–themed flourishes, in addition to people dressed as characters. The maze remained up for a week after the event so that patrons who hadn't attended could explore it as well.

Forrester reports that the maze took a long time to assemble; prep work on the boxes took around twenty hours, and set-up took an additional ten hours of steady work by five people. Still, it was worth it, with Forrester noting that "from a numbers view it was gratifying to have 300+ people come to the after-hours party. But it was even more satisfying to see the smiles, hear the laughter, and watch our customers find joy in exploring the maze" (Forrester 2015).

Broke Hall Community Primary School in Ipswich, England, involved the whole school community in preparation for its Olympics. Each grade level was assigned a different duty, from setting up the Olympic Village to landscaping to keeping athletes healthy, and these duties drove the grade's participation in the event. In addition to this, individual classes selected countries to represent and developed displays with information and trivia about their places. Supplemental themed activities were planned, such as athlete visits and special assemblies. At the end, parents were invited to see their children's work and explore what the school had been working on. In her article about this project, Jayne Gould writes, "And in true British fashion the original date for sports day was rained off, but the next day was fine and the whole school came together to take part in their own version of the Games!" (2012).

Choosing Your Game Type

The game types and examples listed above are certainly not the only options to choose from when you begin to plan how your game will go. Whatever game type or format you choose will reflect your library, your community, and your goals for your project. Keep in mind that the type of game you choose will send indirect messages to your patrons about your intentions. For example, the game One Night: Ultimate Werewolf encourages its players to work together to determine which players are werewolves and which are villagers, and the gameplay encourages skepticism and privileges discussion and analysis. Research backs up the idea that discussion among group members makes it easier to sort out who is lying, and this work in groups is a take-away of playing this particular game (Beck 2015). You will want to think carefully about your goals for the project and about your patrons. There may be themes in your community or school that you can draw on to make your project shine. Above all, a successful project will highlight your services and your library's achievements, and it will celebrate your particular space and community. The case study in textbox 6.1 gives a more detailed example of a successful gaming project.

The Library Stars Tour and Game Type

The Library Stars Tour is structured as a scavenger hunt—students work individually or in groups, traveling around the library to find answers to the questions. This format is appropriate to the goals of the tour, which include

- Introducing students to library faces and spaces
- Helping students feel more comfortable using the library
- Showing students whom they can talk to and where they can go if they realize they have research questions

In particular, since students will not have had library instruction during the course of their introductory writing semester, the tour focuses on getting students into the library and on rewarding them for being there. The structure and design of the tour is a direct result of the goals and objectives driving the game.

TEXTBOX 6.1

CASE STUDY:
BATTLE OF THE BOOKS IN THE
MERCED UNION HIGH SCHOOL DISTRICT

Late one Friday afternoon on a clear day in January 2016, the library at Golden Valley High School in Merced, California, was packed. Students and teachers milled about in groups, chatting, cramming, and waiting. Teams wore shirts they had designed and produced for the occasion. It was time for the annual Battle of the Books competition in the high school district.

Organizers of Merced's Battle of the Books (http://muhsdbattleofthebooks. weebly.com/)—teacher librarians at the schools in the district—identify a number of books (some young adult, and some high school classics like *To Kill a Mockingbird* and *Cannery Row*) and then students and faculty read them and compete in teams to answer questions. The team with the most correct answers wins. Competition pits two teams against each other at once, and teams rotate through several rounds of play.

Anthony Doyle, a teacher librarian at nearby El Capitan High School, has been involved with this project for years. Originally inspired by a California School Library Association presentation given by middle-school teacher librarians who had organized teams for America's Battle of the Books (www.battleofthe-books.org/), teacher librarians in various Merced Union High School District schools began to think about ways they could use the idea in their district. "I didn't do anything with [the project] right away," says Doyle. "A few years later remedial/support English teachers at Livingston High School [another school in the district] wanted to incorporate more reading. The curriculum was heavy on direct instruction and wasn't always engaging for the kids. The reading list for America's Battle of the Books was not appropriate to those students, so I picked some hi-lo titles. It was a huge success, and we ran it for several years" (Doyle 2015).

They revived the program later on, after the district considered eliminating teacher librarian positions, in an effort, according to Doyle, "to raise our visibility in the district and community and show what we do for kids." They decided to stick with their previous tradition of choosing books to fit their student population, and they have had positive feedback and participation since then.

Over the years, the project has remained fundamentally the same, although organizers now use Google Docs and Google Forms rather than paper. In the 2016 iteration, twenty teams participated, with almost one hundred individuals taking part. Organizers discuss the project through e-mail, texting, and Google Docs, and everyone pitches in where they can. Some years Battle of the Books has been integrated into the curriculum at various sites.

Doyle notes that if you choose to take on this kind of project, "either start small or don't try to do it alone. With six of us working together, it is still almost overwhelming." That being said, it remains a worthy event. "I think we reach a part of the student population that doesn't get involved in too many activities and don't always feel connected to the school," Doyle says. "It's nice to give them that connection" (2015).

⑥ Key Points

This chapter focused on highlighting different games and game types. As you think about your own library's particular context and situation, you will want to also consider what type of game might best fit your purposes. There are many game examples listed here, and depending on your needs, you may find inspiration in one (or several!) as you think about your goals. Overall, you will want to make sure that the game you plan reflects the needs of your patrons, your library, and your community.

- When you plan your game, think about the interplay of the following at your library:
  - Library partners and stakeholders
  - Library (and patron) goals
  - Your audience of potential players and participants
  - What you hope your audience will know as a result of playing your game
  - How you will design your game
  - What you want your audience to remember

- Take inspiration from the work others have done in terms of game design and implementation—you don't have to reinvent the wheel.
- Consider the advantages and disadvantages of different types of games (such as scavenger hunts, board games, video games, and role-playing games) when you plan your own project.

In the next chapter, you will learn how games and game projects fit within the context of library instruction.

⑥ References

American Heritage Dictionary of the English Language. 2015. Houghton Mifflin Harcourt. https://ahdictionary.com/word/search.html?q=game.

Bailin, Kylie. 2015. "From 'The Research Games' to Tours: The Evolution of First Year Orientation Activities." *College & Research Libraries News* 76, no. 11 (December): 586–89.

Beck, Donna, Rachel Callison, John Fudrow, and Dan Hood. 2008. "Your Library Instruction Is in Another Castle: Developing Information Literacy Based Video Games at Carnegie Mellon University." In *Gaming in Academic Libraries: Collections, Marketing, and Information Literacy*, edited by Amy Harris and Scott E. Rice, 135–48. Chicago: Association of College and Research Libraries.

Beck, Julie. 2015. "Groups Are Better Than Individuals at Sniffing Out Lies." *Atlantic.* www.theatlantic.com/health/archive/2015/09/groups-are-better-than-individuals-at-sniffing-out-lies/405244/#article-comments.

Cannon, L. H., and Susan M. Blackman. 2000. "Reenacting the Titanic: A Simulation Game Teaches Lifelong Lessons." *Voice of Youth Advocates* 23, no. 3 (August): 176–77.

Carnes, Mark C. 2014. *Minds on Fire: How Role-Immersion Games Transform College.* Cambridge, MA: Harvard University Press.

Danforth, Liz. 2011. "Why Game Learning Works (Games, Gamers, & Gaming)." *Library Journal* 136 (7): 67.

Doyle, Anthony. 2016. In an e-mail to the author, February 2.

Entertainment Software Association. 2015. *Essential Facts about the Computer and Video Game Industry*. www.theesa.com/wp-content/uploads/2015/04/ESA-Essential-Facts-2015.pdf.

Flegal, Sabrina, and Kathryn Schweers. 2014. "Library Survivor." *Library Media Connection* 32, no. 6 (May): 18.

Fleming, Laura. 2016. Worlds of Learning. www.worlds-of-learning-nmhs.com/.

Forrester, Amy Seto. 2015. "An A-Maze-ing Library Experience." Association for Library Service to Children Blog. www.alsc.ala.org/blog/2015/11/an-a-maze-ing-library-experience/.

Fuerste-Henry, Andrew, and Sarah F. Smith. 2015. "Why Should Kids Have All the Fun?" *Library Journal* 140, no. 3 (February): 23.

Gould, Jayne. 2012. "Our Whole School Olympics Project: Love Sport: Love Reading." *School Librarian* 60, no. 3 (Autumn): 140.

Hertz, Daniel. 2016. "What Computer Games Taught Me About Urban Planning." *Atlantic*. www.theatlantic.com/business/archive/2016/02/urban-planning-computer-games/470895/.

Hudson-Vitale, Cynthia, and Jennifer Moore. 2016. "Digital Badges." *College & Research Libraries News* 77, no. 2 (February): 70–73.

Hurst, Carol Otis. 1996. "'Grab a Book' Game." *Teaching Pre K–8* 26 (May): 84–87.

Markey, Karen, Fritz Swanson, and Andrea Jenkins et al. 2008. "The Effectiveness of a Web-Based Board Game for Teaching Undergraduate Students Information Literacy Concepts and Skills." *D-Lib Magazine* 14, nos. 9 and 10.

Mayer, Brian, and Christopher Harris. 2009. *Libraries Got Game: Aligned Learning through Modern Board Games*. Chicago, IL: American Library Association Editions.

McCain, Cheryl. 2007. "Scavenger Hunt Assignments in Academic Libraries: Viewpoints versus Reality." *College & Undergraduate Libraries* 14 (1): 19–31.

O'Hanlon, Nancy, Karen Diaz, and Fred Roecker. 2009. "A Game-Based Multimedia Approach to Library Orientation." *Loex Conference Proceedings 2007*, paper 19. http://commons.emich.edu/loexconf2007/19.

Quinney, Kayla L., Sara D. Smith, and Quinn Galbraith. 2010. "Bridging the Gap: Self-Directed Staff Technology Training." *Information Technology & Libraries* 29, no. 4 (December): 205–13.

Rice, Scott, and Margaret Gregor. 2010. "The Library Adventure Game." *School Library Journal* 56, no. 8 (August): 22–23.

Ries-Taggart, Jennifer. 2010. "LARP! @ Your Library." *Public Libraries* 49, no. 1 (January): 7–8.

Robbins, M. Brandon. 2015. "Adults Only." *Library Journal* 140, no. 9 (May): 51–51.

Rosenstein, Jennifer. 2013. "Ghost Hunters in the Library: Using an Interactive Mystery Game for Freshman Library Orientation." *College & Research Libraries News* 74, no. 7 (July): 350–53.

Rutherford, Emily, Katharina Freund, Heather Jenks, and Inger Mewburn. 2015. "Badging the Library: Are Digital Badges the Next Innovation for Library Skills and Training?" https://digitalcollections.anu.edu.au/bitstream/1885/13234/3/Rutherford%20et%20al%20Badging%20the%20library%202015.pdf.

Smale, Maura A. 2011. "Learning through Quests and Contests: Games in Information Literacy Instruction." *Journal of Library Innovation* 2 (2): 36–55.

Stahura, Dawn and Erin Milanese. 2013. "Teaching with Zombies: Bringing Information Literacy Back from the Dead." *College & Research Libraries News* 74 (7): 354–56.

Sullivan, Dean, and Jessica Critten. 2014. "Adventures in Research Creating a Video Game Textbook for an Information Literacy Course." *College & Research Libraries News* 75 (10): 570–73.

Using Games in Instruction

LIBRARIANS WHO PROVIDE instruction to students and patrons at schools, colleges, and public libraries are all too familiar with the pitfalls of lecture-based teaching. On one hand, there is so much information to cover, and lectures can seem like the most efficient method of sharing that information with students. On the other hand, students frequently disengage when faced with the prospect of yet another informational session. How to balance this need to disseminate information with the need for students to engage with the material can be the source of headaches.

While games by themselves cannot act as panaceas, they can work to help connect students with material, and they may provide modest gains in information retention. Games can help, in other words, but reframing your material in a game context will not necessarily make it more understandable or useful.

In a study that examined the impact of educational video games on Saudi kindergarteners' retention of English words, the author speculates that it is possible that students responded in part to the "richer content with audio, video and animation which was provided through Video Games" (AlShaiji 2015, 129). The study showed that children who learned vocabulary through video games retained more than children who learned through more traditional methods. Furthermore, Larysa Naldony and Andrea Halabi (2016) found that when they incorporated elements of games into the structure of a large lecture course, students were more engaged, demonstrated high participation levels, and attended the class more frequently than before. These gains were observed across ages and genders.

Games can wake up a class and involve them more directly in the goals of the session, especially when the included game elements reflect and provide a complement to what is being taught. While games in a library session should not be used to complicate materials or to provide simple entertainment, they can be a beneficial addition to a classroom setting. In other words, games can help students better understand material—but you should not gamify simply because you can.

Integrating games and game elements into library instruction sessions can be a delicate process, and this chapter will focus on ways you might do so by complementing the material you are teaching. Although games can (and should) make learning enjoyable and relevant, care should be taken to ensure that they serve a purpose within the instructional context of a class and that their use reflects the outcomes you are hoping to achieve from instruction. Games deployed strategically and thoughtfully can be of great benefit to both your students and the library.

⌾ Games and Instruction

Anyone who has watched library instruction session students sit up a little straighter when a game is introduced knows that games can have an impact on engagement. But can they actually help students learn? Much has been written about how video games, in particular, are able to provide immersive experiences for their players, requiring them to complete numerous essential tasks in order to move forward. Some of these tasks are tedious but must be completed in order to get through the game. In *Everything Bad Is Good for You: How Today's Popular Culture Is Actually Making Us Smarter*, Steven Johnson writes,

> The dirty little secret of gaming is how much time you spend not having fun. You may be frustrated; you may be confused or disoriented; you may be stuck. When you put the game down and move back into the real world, you may find yourself mentally working through the problem you've been wrestling with, as though you were worrying a loose tooth. . . . Who wants to escape to a world that irritates you 90 percent of the time? (2005, 25–26)

And yet, as Johnson goes on to point out, millions of people keep playing video games, despite the fact that they are often frustrating. Johnson ties this phenomenon to the ability of games to "tap into the brain's natural reward circuitry" (2005, 34). Games are able to push their players onward by constantly giving them small rewards and instilling them with the desire to see what can happen in the virtual world, and what will happen next. Although there may be some differences between player engagement with video games and engagement with other types of games, the potential parallels with instruction and learning here are clear.

Of course, however, library instruction and video games also have key differences. One of these is time—library instruction sessions are often limited to one class session, and librarians don't have enough time as it is to let students work to tease out meaning and database nuances on their own. It can seem daunting even to provide a basic introduction to database structure and resources that are available through the library. That being said, games can be used to help involve students in the session and to help them begin to understand some of the essential structures of the tools they are using.

Curtis Chandler (2013) argues that instructors looking to incorporate game aspects into instruction should think about the following game dynamics.

Narrative context. Braiding the choices presented to game players into a coherent storyline that allows students the chance to both experiment and learn without excessive risk of failure and to follow along with a narrative.

Explicit interconnectedness. Using rules to guide player behavior and help players achieve their goals rather than using them in a more punitive way, and making connections between various game tasks to avoid the perception that they are arbitrary.

Well-ordered problems. Scaffolding activities so that they teach essential skills as the game progresses.

Control and choice. Letting players make their own decisions that have various consequences, thus giving them a degree of control over what happens during the game.

Customization and co-design. Granting players the opportunity to tailor the game to their own needs and preferences, providing them with more autonomy and engagement.

These principles, pulled from the design of successful video games, can go a long way toward encouraging students to invest the same level of energy in their learning that they do when playing games. In short, they have the potential to let learning feel more like a game, which folds its instructional aspects into its play, than like sitting and listening to a lecture. This can also help to provide students with incentive to keep pushing forward in their studies. It should also be noted that there is no imperative to make games used in library instruction exactly like those sold for commercial purposes. The idea here is to take inspiration from the success of video games and incorporate elements that make sense in the context of library instruction, not to copy them wholesale.

In addition, designing an entire library instruction session around the lessons pulled from video games is very difficult. It may even be impossible to fully structure a session like this, and the time and energy required to fully develop a game-based instruction session may or may not pay off in terms of student information retention. For example, in a study that measured whether playing computer-based adventure games leads to better problem-solving skills, it was unclear whether students transferred skills over to use in other contexts, and thus the authors concluded that it would be inadvisable to depend on these sorts of games as a way to build problem-solving skills (Curtis and Lawson 2002).

But there is some evidence that game-based instruction can be beneficial and can encourage students to take away more than they would from more run-of-the-mill instruction. In a study focused on risk-based learning games, Ian M. Devonshire and colleagues found that small levels of risk (e.g., allowing students to bet tokens based on how confident they were in their quiz answers) may engage students more fully and may push them to keep thinking about course lessons for a longer period of time. In the study, although quiz scores from directly after the instruction session were similar for the risk group (which also offered small prizes as incentives) and other groups, scores from quizzes taken later showed improvement (Devonshire et al. 2014).

It should be noted as well that games do not need to take up an entire library instruction session—on the contrary, it is quite possible to incorporate a few small games and still have time to provide more traditional direct instruction. Depending on how much time you have to work with your students, you may decide to start with a game, use a game in the middle of the session to gauge understanding, or spend a few minutes at the end of the session using games to reinforce what students have learned. Even games that only last a few minutes can go a long way toward more fully engaging students, especially if they appeal to students' intrinsic motivation and align with the goals of the class.

⊚ Aligning Games to Instruction Goals

Though games can be beneficial and can work actively to engage students with the substance of your lesson, they need to align coherently with the goals and outcomes you are hoping to achieve. While games for their own sake may be entertaining, they will not be as productive in terms of generating student interest and engagement in the library. Setting goals to dovetail with outcomes is covered more thoroughly elsewhere in this book, but a brief refresher is provided here. When you think about your game's goals, you will want to consider the following.

- What interests or needs do your students have? For example, is there an assignment they are working on? Are there important skill sets being reinforced by library instruction?
- Will you meet with these students just once? Or will there be other opportunities to work with them in the future?
- What goals do you have for the instruction session?
- What goals does the course instructor have for the instruction session?

It may also be helpful to think about how you will define success in the context of your instruction. Will students complete a quiz at the end that shows they have understood the material? Will you later collect and evaluate materials to see if they have incorporated what you discussed? Your definition of success for instruction will help to determine whether or not you met your goals and will help guide the outcomes you see as necessary. Planning from the start to meet your goals will go a long way in helping you achieve them.

⊚ Types of Games for Instruction

While there are a great many different types of games that could fit feasibly within the context of the library, instruction provides its own challenges and may not be suitable for every type of game. As you plan, you will want to think about how your game will fit with your instruction plans. For example, many games played during class times are about 10–20 minutes long. Though this time span folds easily into longer class periods, if you only have a 50-minute session, it can easily eat up more time than may be available.

Depending on your goals and context, you may choose to use a game that takes the place of an instruction session or one that uses the whole session. In the case of a game that takes the place of more formal instruction, it is essential to make sure that the information you need students to understand is baked into the game's plan and that all students have enough time to finish before the session ends. It is also important to think about accommodations for students with disabilities—your game should include everyone in the class and not leave anyone out. Types of games that may work within a library instruction session include

- Scavenger hunts/mystery games where students gather clues or artifacts from various library spaces
- Quiz-style games—many librarians have experimented with Jeopardy!-style frameworks, and these can also be adapted to fit the needs of your students. Con-

sider, for example, asking students to work in teams to answer the quiz questions rather than rewarding just one person

- Trivia games where students receive points for sharing their knowledge
- Computer or video-based games
- Collaborative games where students work together to solve problems
- Competitive games

While each of these game types has its own strengths and challenges, perhaps the most important part of selecting what style of game you will use is deciding how well it will mesh within your established context. Questions you may use to guide your way include

- How much time do I have with this group of students?
- What do the students already know?
- What do I want them to know?
- Are there particular research goals I would like to emphasize? (For example, finding help in the library, or working with classmates in teams to accomplish goals.)
- Will I meet with these students again?
- What interests or needs do these students have that can be fulfilled by their participation in this game?
- Will students have time to participate in a debriefing session after the game? If not, is this essential?

If you are working, for example, with students who have been to the library before, it may not be as important for them to receive a run-down of how to navigate library spaces. On the other hand, if your instruction takes the form of a library orientation for new students early in the school year, you may want to provide this information in order to make the next few years easier.

Flipped Instruction

It can sometimes be beneficial to use the concept of flipped instruction when planning your game or activity. Flipped instruction means that students complete an assignment—often this can involve listening to a recorded lecture, or completing a quiz or brief tutorial—before they arrive in the library. Flipped instruction takes a bit of extra planning and work since the materials need to be ready before it happens, but it can also shave minutes from needed instruction by providing students with some context before they arrive. In addition, students who have already completed the assignment are ready to start to talk about the concepts of the session and have had time to begin to organize their thought in advance. In particular, flipped instruction can be a good way to introduce concepts and allow students to begin to work with different databases so they are not lost when they arrive in class.

Despite its benefits, there are also some potential challenges to flipped instruction. One is that it only will work if students complete the assignments ahead of time. This will often require you to communicate with the faculty member or classroom teacher for the students so you can ask them whether they are willing to assign the material. In addition, students who are not receiving any credit or points for completing the material may decide to ignore it. This can be tricky since librarians often do not teach semester-long courses or assign grades. Some discussion between you and the faculty member or teacher may be necessary beforehand. A potential e-mail script you can use when communicating with educational partners is shown in the textbox.

Prior communication can go a long way toward smoothing the planning process and opening up space in the time available for instruction so you can incorporate games and other activities. If you are thinking of using flipped instruction, the following checklist may help you to ensure that everything is ready to go.

√ Flipped instruction materials (recorded lectures, quizzes, tutorial notes, etc.) are ready (this can often take longer than it might appear at first—planning ahead is a good idea).
√ There has been communication between the library and the classroom teacher or faculty member about whether flipped instruction materials can be sent to students.
√ Materials have been assigned to students, either directly or by asking a teacher or faculty member to assign them.
√ Students have some incentive to complete the materials (this can be a short quiz, a direct connection to the material that will be covered, or an upcoming related assignment).
√ You have a Plan B to use in case something happens and you need to provide a quick summary of the flipped instruction materials.

While flipped instruction can be a good way to introduce students to the material before the start of class, it is also a group endeavor—and it won't work unless students do their part.

Using Games to Get to Know Students

Icebreaker games can be helpful in establishing a productive tone in an instruction session and in introducing concepts and topics that will be discussed in more detail later. Because you may be meeting with a class whose members are already familiar with each other, it may not be necessary to have students provide basic introductions. However, since the class is probably new to you (and vice versa!) it can be helpful to start the session with a sort of introductory activity. The activities listed below have been used successfully by librarians before and may provide inspiration for ways you might think about getting started in your own instruction sessions.

Tinkertoy Towers

This activity can help set the stage for students to work in functioning teams and can encourage them to appreciate the roles and contributions of each team member. As students enter the room, each one receives a predetermined number of Tinkertoy pieces. Initially, students try to build structures with their own pieces. Later, they reconvene with group members to see what they can build by working together, and this can lead into a discussion of what they gained from their work as a team, and how teams can work most effectively (Jones 2011, 11–13).

Jeopardy!-Style Games

Many students and teachers are already familiar with the Jeopardy! game-show format, and it can easily be adapted for use as a library instruction session opener. An added benefit to this is that the game can serve as a method for learning about what students already know about the library, and it can be an introduction to the types of information they will encounter during the session. Magolis and Neyer (2011) provide as possible categories Our Library, Scholarly Journals, Library Databases, Searching Basics, and Citation Stuff. Templates for the game can be found online, and it is easy to adapt it using PowerPoint for use in library instruction.

Working with Teachers and Professors

In school and academic libraries, many library instruction sessions come about because teachers and professors want them for their classes. Although librarians have been able to make inroads in recent years into teaching for-credit information literacy classes, these classes still do not represent the large part of library instruction. Therefore, it is a good idea to give some thought to the best way to connect with teachers and professors at your school or institution.

There is more information elsewhere in this book about working with project partners and stakeholders, and much of this can apply to working relationships between teachers and professors and librarians as well. As in so many other instances, communication between the library and the teacher or professor is essential to creating games in library instruction that meet the needs of all parties. Even if you will be the primary facilitator of the game during the session itself, it is a good idea to let the instructor know what you plan to do and to make sure that they have no objections, especially in the case of longer games (e.g., scavenger hunts or group activities that last longer than a quick Jeopardy!-style review). Questions to kick start communications with teachers about incorporating games into library instruction might include

- What is the goal of the game?
- How will the game meet the instructor's goals for the class session?
- How will the game meet the library's goals for the class session?
- How long will the game take?
- How will you measure student learning?
- What back-up activities do you have in case there is an issue with the game?

Textbox 7.2 is a template you might use or adapt when beginning the conversation about games in the context of the library with teachers or faculty members.

POSSIBLE TEMPLATE FOR STARTING A CONVERSATION WITH FACULTY ABOUT GAMES IN INSTRUCTION

I have been doing some research into the benefits of using games to engage students and would like to try out a game format for the first half of the library session. I have been looking over your instruction request, and I see that one of your goals for the session is that students know how to find both print and database materials they can use. The game I have been designing would give students first-hand knowledge of how to search in the library's holdings, and it would show them exactly what they need to do to access the materials they need. If you would prefer not to use a game format for the session, just let me know. If you'd like more information, I would also be happy to meet with you to talk about what I have come up with, or we could work together to plan an alternative. Thank you for considering my proposal. I'm looking forward to working with your students.

Your game has a much better chance at success if it addresses the teacher's goals for the session and provides a means by which students can attain learning outcomes. Careful thought about how the game fits within the class and the library session, coupled with constructive communication with class instructors, can go a long way toward smoothing your game's reception with both students and school partners.

Assessment

Assessing your game will play a key role in both its success and your understanding of it. Assessment will also help you build a case for your game's utility and purpose within the context of library instruction. Games that can show evidence that they contribute to student learning are much more likely to be embraced by teachers, faculty, and libraries alike. More about assessment can be found elsewhere in this book; however, it is important in this context to keep several points in mind.

Authentic Assessment vs. Traditional Assessment

Authentic assessment measures student success by examining artifacts they have produced to show their understanding. Authentic assessment can be performed using student papers, for example, or by observing students while they complete a task. Generally, performance is measured via a rubric that assigns and explains scores based on proficiency level (Mueller 2014).

Traditional assessment, on the other hand, asks students to complete a quiz or test that determines their understanding based on their answers. Illustrating the difference between the two, Jon Mueller writes,

> To use a silly example, if I had to choose a chauffeur from between someone who passed the *driving* portion of the driver's license test but failed the *written* portion, or someone who failed the driving portion and passed the written portion, I would choose the driver

who most directly demonstrated the ability to drive . . . however, I would *prefer* a driver who passed both portions. (2014)

There is definitely room for both kinds of assessment in the context of library instruction. You may end up using both kinds at various points as you implement and evaluate your game.

Student Feedback

In addition to assessment that measures skill attainment as a result of your game, it is also a good idea to run the game by some students to gauge whether or not they will enjoy it. Games should be enjoyable for their players, even in (maybe especially in) an educational setting. Games that seem fun to librarians may or may not pass muster with their intended players, so it is good to ask students beforehand for their thoughts.

In an academic library or school library with student assistants, it is not difficult to ask students to try out a game or meet with you to discuss your plan beforehand. Offering food can encourage people to share their thoughts. In a primary school library, it may be more difficult to attain student feedback, so you may try the game first with a small group of students before launching it outright.

Questions you might ask students participating in focus groups or completing the game on a trial basis may include

- Did you like the game?
- Were you able to complete the game?
- How long did it take you to complete?
- Was there anything that was unclear or that you had trouble understanding?
- Did you think _____ (a part of the game intended to be funny) was funny?
- Do you think other students would enjoy playing this game?
- Would you like to play the game again?
- Do you have any suggestions or other feedback that hasn't been covered?

Devoting time and thought to the question of how your game will be received by students is essential toward ensuring it will have a good reception and that it can accomplish its goals. Positive assessment also gives you good talking points to use when working with faculty and encouraging them to help you implement games during library instruction.

Examples of Instructional Games

The Amazing Race Game at McConnell Library, Radford University

Realizing that students found second-year library instruction sessions to be too similar to those they'd taken during their first year, librarians at McConnell Library of Radford University began looking for ways to shake things up. Since they generally teach about 75 sections of this course during the fall semester and another 10–15 during the spring semester, there were potentially many students who could benefit from some change. Inspiration came in the form of a presentation by Katherine O'Clair at LOEX of the West (now Library Instruction West) in 2012. O'Clair presented on a game idea she described as "loosely based on *The Amazing Race*," a TV show, which promised more student engagement and a much more active instruction experience (http://lgdata. s3-website-us-east-1.amazonaws.com/docs/1000/475218/LOTW2012_The_Amazing_Library_Race_OClair.pdf). O'Clair's game was based, in turn, on one created for use in a Freshman Learning Community by Jennifer Duvernay at Arizona State (O'Clair 2012). The game's many possible iterations speak to how adaptable it is to various purposes and underline its potential for use in instruction sessions, orientations, and beyond.

Candice Benjes-Small, the head of Information Literacy and Outreach at McConnell Library, worked with colleagues to shape their own Amazing Race game. Radford University's Amazing Race game used the established game structure but adapted its content to fit the objectives of a required course generally taken during students' sophomore year.

The game at Radford is played in teams during the course of a fifty-minute library instruction session and takes place in several rounds. In each round, teams receive an envelope with questions in five different areas: background research, scholarly articles, SuperSearch, APA, and annotated bibliographies. Resources that can be used to answer the questions for each round are located on a LibGuide (McConnell Library 2016) that students consult during the course of the session (http://libguides.radford.edu/c. php?g=166662&p=1093552). Once a team completes one round, they return their envelope, check their answers, and receive the next envelope to move on. Teams that finish early get to leave early, which Benjes-Small says usually provides ample incentive to keep students motivated. Generally, students are able to finish easily during the fifty-minute time frame.

One benefit to the game is its prep time: though Benjes-Small says that while it initially took about four hours to plan and set up, now that it is established, librarians only spend one hour per semester updating it and making sure everything is working. At a library that sees 450 instruction sessions each academic year, with some instruction librarians teaching forty-five classes per semester, this is no small accomplishment. In addition, students seem to really enjoy the game, and it can be especially fun for both students and librarians when it gets competitive.

Radford librarians completed some assessment of the game, gathering annotated bibliographies from students who played during library instruction and students who instead attended a flipped library instruction session, which is another option available to professors who bring their students to the library. They could find no appreciable differences in student learning between the two groups, which speaks to the game's effectiveness. Faculty members also expressed satisfaction with the game and indicated that students seemed to be getting the information they needed from it.

Benjes-Small (2016) recommends that librarians planning similar games should make sure to coordinate with professors at their institutions; for example, to see if they mind letting students out early as an incentive. She also cautions that as with any game or program, there should be some consideration of ADA compliance to ensure that students with physical disabilities are not placed at a disadvantage.

The RADAR Challenge at Loyola Marymount University

Librarians at Loyola Marymount had an established worksheet activity for use with students in one of their core courses, but they found that engagement could be low, and that some students stopped working altogether without finishing. Recognizing the importance of the concepts in the original (which emphasized using rationale, authority, date, accuracy, and relevance (RADAR) to establish source credibility), Instructional Design Librarian Lindsey McLean thought about ways she could keep the substance of the activity but reformat it in a way that would motivate students to keep pushing forward. Though at first she considered using an established game format, like Jeopardy! for example, reflection on the outcomes for the course convinced her to go in a different direction. "I wanted a totally new type of game," she says (2016).

This lead to the RADAR Challenge (http://electra.lmu.edu/TheRadarGame/story.html), a game completed during library instruction sessions as a way to get students thinking about sources. During a typical session, students form teams, pick a challenge from one of three categories (science, social science, and the humanities), and then work to answer questions about the various sources. The questions come largely from the original worksheet activity, although they are now accompanied by multiple-choice answer options and hosted in Articulate Storyline, a software for developing interactive, online learning content. Students have four chances to try to answer correctly, and they get different numbers of points (and different detailed graphics of stars) depending on how quickly they pick the right answer. Points are tallied on a white board, which can give students more motivation to try to answer correctly. McLean says that some faculty members give additional rewards to game winners, such as extra credit or their choice of when they will give presentations, but that the stars often seem like plenty of incentive. Once students finish (generally in about ten minutes), librarians lead into a discussion about their results, which is enriched by the students' new understanding of the material.

The game took about a week to organize, partly because there were already questions available to use from the original worksheet activity and because McLean was already familiar with the format she wanted to use. Periodically there are revisions, such as including more than one challenge article, which can take a bit longer to implement. Librarians at Loyola Marymount make use of frequent surveys to ensure that players and faculty members are happy with how the game is going. McLean reports that a "vast majority" of students like it and say it helps them understand the material (2016).

McLean emphasizes that gamification isn't just sticking content into a framework that already exists—it is about tailoring game objectives to meet learning outcomes and the needs of a particular population. For instance, the RADAR Challenge was designed specifically to be an activity completed by students during scheduled library instruction sessions. Though it can be completed successfully outside this context, the total game experience is tied to its environment. McLean advises librarians interested in establishing similar activities in their libraries to

1. Focus on the objective of the activity and design from there, much as you would when planning instruction sessions.
2. Think about how the game exists and the context it will reside in (a personality quiz completed online, for example, versus a game completed in teams to find information).
3. Use elements of motivation to encourage players to complete the tasks the game asks of them. (2016)

McLean also notes she is happy to share raw files for use with Articulate Storyline with others who are interested in adapting the game to their own contexts.

The Library Stars Tour and Instruction

The Library Stars Tour's design reflects its intended use as a replacement for more formal library instruction sessions and its role as a complement to instruction in introductory writing courses. It can be completed independently by students, and instructors have leeway to determine when in the semester it will be assigned. Its twin purposes of providing information about the library and its services and establishing the library as a comfortable, welcoming venue for student research are similar to those that might be seen in a more formal instruction setting. The main aims of the tour are

- To teach students about library spaces and services
- To help students navigate the library on their own
- To develop and nurture library relationships with faculty members who will ask students to complete the tour
- To give students the impression of the library as a welcoming space that exists to a large degree to help them with their research

The tour is designed to fit within the curriculum of introductory writing classes at the university and to provide a supplement to them—for this reason, good communication with faculty members is important. The tour's structure as a scavenger hunt–type activity means that it is fairly easy to make changes to it every semester, or to customize according to class. If there is a particular class, for example, whose professor wants an extra question about APA formatting, it is possible to work with this professor to add a question that will address his or her needs (though it will be important to make sure that all versions of the tour include this extra question).

Additionally, the tour provides a base of information that the library can draw on in the future to ground additional library instruction sessions. While it may be impossible to ensure that every student on campus will take the tour, it is possible to reach a great many more students than would learn about the library without it, and this helps knowledge of library services and practices become more a part of the culture of the school as a whole.

Like many other instruction-based games and game activities, the Library Stars Tour largely reflects its context within the university and the curriculum. While it attempts to provide students with a fun and interactive introduction to library spaces and services, it does not lose sight of its primary goals, which drive its content and structure.

Key Points

This chapter discussed ways you can plan, structure, and implement game activities during library instruction. It bears repeating that your experience using games during instruction will depend largely on your library, your relationship with teachers or faculty, your students, and the needs of a particular class. Games can take the form of short reviews completed before or after the meat of the session, or of longer, structured activities. Your use of games will reflect your library, your goals, and your students.

- Games can enhance instruction and help students retain material.
- Games should reflect the goals of the session—for example, if you are discussing information literacy, then any games you use should in some way reinforce the properties you are hoping students will take away.

- Flipped models of instruction can help you prepare students for a game and also free up precious instruction minutes that can be used more actively.
- You will need to establish respectful, open relationships with teachers and faculty at your institution in order to get them on board with game use during library instruction.
- Assessment of student artifacts, in addition to quiz and test results and student feedback, will give you your clearest view of how your game is received—which lets you adapt it to better fit your needs.
- The Library Stars Tour works to meet the needs of faculty members and the student body at large by serving as a proxy for more traditional library instruction and by reflecting the direct needs of students and faculty members for introductory writing courses.

In the next chapter, you will learn about how you can make your game accessible to all patrons, in addition to challenges that may arise due to the digital divide.

References

AlShaiji, Ohoud Abdullatif. 2015. "Video Games Promote Saudi Children's English Vocabulary Retention." *Education* 136, no. 2 (Winter): 123–32.

Benjes-Small, Candice. 2016. Phone conversation with the author, March 11.

Chandler, Curtis. 2013. "The Use of Game Dynamics to Enhance Curriculum and Instruction: What Teachers Can Learn from the Design of Video Games." *Journal of Curriculum & Instruction* 6, no. 2 (March): 60–75.

Curtis, David D., and Mike J. Lawson. 2002. "Computer Adventure Games as Problem-Solving Environments." *International Education Journal* 3, no. 4 (November): 43–56.

Devonshire, Ian M., Jenny Davis, and Sophie Fairweather et al. 2014. "Risk-Based Learning Games Improve Long-Term Retention of Information among School Pupils." *Plos One* 9, no. 7 (July): 1–9.

Johnson, Steven. 2005. *Everything Bad Is Good for You: How Today's Popular Culture Is Actually Making Us Smarter.* New York: Riverhead Books.

Jones, Jen. 2011. "Tinkertoy Towers: Building Research Projects in Teams." In *Let the Games Begin! Engaging Students with Field-Tested Interactive Information Literacy Instruction*, edited by Theresa R. McDevitt, 11–13. New York: Neal-Schuman Publishers.

Magolis, David, and Linda Neyer. 2011. "Let's Play Information Literacy Jeopardy!" In *Let the Games Begin! Engaging Students with Field-Tested Interactive Information Literacy Instruction*, edited by Theresa R. McDevitt, 6–8. New York: Neal-Schuman Publishers.

McConnell Library, Radford University. 2016. Core 201—Amazing Race: Home. http://libguides.radford.edu/CORE201AR.

McLean, Lindsay. 2016. Phone conversation with the author, March 16.

Mueller, Jon. 2014. Authentic Assessment Toolbox. http://jfmueller.faculty.noctrl.edu/toolbox/whatisit.htm.

Naldony, Larysa, and Andrea Halabi. 2016. "Student Participation and Achievement in a Large Lecture Course with Game-Based Learning." *Simulation and Gaming* 47, no. 1 (February): 51–72.

O'Clair, Katherine. 2012. "The Amazing Library Race." Presentation at LOEX of the West, Burbank, California, June 6–8. http://lgdata.s3-website-us-east-1.amazonaws.com/docs/1000/475218/LOTW2012_The_Amazing_Library_Race_OClair.pdf.

Game Accessibility

IT IS IMPORTANT for your game to be accessible to patrons, full stop. If patrons cannot complete your game, they won't, and you will lose the opportunity to connect with them. Furthermore, the Americans with Disabilities Act (ADA) requires that you provide equitable access to services for people with disabilities (2009). Happily, there are ways you can work to make sure that all of your patrons have access to your game, and frequently the steps you take to provide access for one group of people will also benefit others.

As you plan, it may be beneficial to think about the distinction between accessibility and accommodation, though these terms are at times used almost interchangeably. Katie Rose Guest Pryal, who has explored this issue in a number of blog posts, describes this difference as follows.

> Accessibility . . . means that a space is always, 100% of the time, welcoming to people with disabilities. Accessibility means that "accommodations" are integrated into a space and are not particularized to an individual—but rather created for our society as a whole. We as a society *are* people with disabilities. Therefore we, as a society, build spaces and procedures *for* people with disabilities. (2016)

Accessibility means that people don't need to ask for additional or alternative services—these services are a part of the whole experience. For example, elevator access to all floors of a building is essential for patrons who use wheelchairs, but it is also helpful for patrons who are visiting with small children or who are carrying heavy books and materials. The elevator is available and patrons do not need to ask to use it—it is an option they can choose to use or not.

Ideally, the structure of your game will be accessible to the widest number of people possible without the need for accommodations that can be implemented only on request.

One of the benefits to using games in the library or classroom is the opportunity to connect with patrons and students in a different way than you might with more traditional approaches.

Certain games involve assumptions about their players that may or may not be true. These assumptions can include that players can easily walk to various locations; that players have access to the technology they need in order to participate; that players can see small print, or distinguish between different colors; or that players feel comfortable approaching strangers to ask questions. Students and patrons who play your game may have learning and physical disabilities, both visible and invisible, and may not have access to the technology you are using to host the activity. It is crucial to take steps to ensure that your game is as inclusive as possible and that it will not alienate the very patrons you are hoping to reach.

While it may ultimately be impossible to ensure that your game can be played the exact same way by every individual, it is certainly possible to plan it in a way that allows participation by a large number of people. Taking time to think about the assumptions you are making as you plan your game can be beneficial. In addition, there are many guidelines and suggestions for increasing your game's accessibility that can be found in books and online. The Association of Specialized and Cooperative Library Agencies (ASCLA), for example, provides a toolkit of materials tailored toward different types of disabilities (www.ala.org/ascla/asclaprotools/accessibilitytipsheets).

Benefits of Accessibility

As mentioned above, in many cases, working to make your game accessible (i.e., planning it in a way that allows participation by as many people as possible without them needing to ask for accommodation) may have benefits for all players. For instance, if you provide paper copies of an online scavenger hunt in order to ensure that students can play without computer access, it is likely that you will help students who benefit from taking notes or from being able to physically touch the game materials in addition to those who may not have the device needed to play the game. Structuring this as a choice players make before beginning the game rather than as an extra they need to ask for helps encourage more participation. Similarly, built-in time for thought before players answer questions may also be beneficial for more introverted players or those who would prefer to consider their options before making a choice.

The Able Gamers Foundation, a nonprofit that focuses on working with video game developers to make games more accessible, has published a guide, "Includification," written by Mark C. Barlet and Steve D. Spohn, that details various video game features that can be used to make gameplay possible for more players. In one section, the authors refer to what they call *baby friendly tests*—settings that allow gameplay without sound. These can be used by new parents with small children in order to play video games while children are asleep. Game play is not negatively affected by not having sound included. Though these settings were developed in order to allow people with hearing disabilities to play, there are benefits to others who do not have these disabilities as well (Barlet and Spohn 2013). Christina C. Wray writes, "The great thing about accessibility is that all learners have a better experience when accessibility features are utilized in online instructional materials to ensure that learners experiencing these barriers have access" (2013, 361).

In some cases, it can be fairly easy to make activities accessible. Videos and computer-based tasks, for example, can make use of optional transcripts and captions that record and describe what is happening on-screen. Similarly, interactive tutorials and other projects can include read-aloud options. Some libraries—if funding allows—have worked to circumvent technology-access issues by providing iPads or other devices for checkout at the circulation desk, expanding participation beyond the owners of particular devices. Building these into the activity as choices players can make as they complete a game is essential—whenever possible, patrons should not have to explain their need for accommodation or ask for alternative arrangements.

In "Museums and Technology: Being Inclusive Helps Accessibility for All," several disability-and-access practitioners who also have disabilities discuss what accessibility means to them and how a lack of it can create barriers. The article is made up of different sections that discuss the individual experiences of the various authors. Though museums and libraries provide different services, the experiences of patrons with disabilities at museums may be instructive. In the article, Kirsten Hearn writes,

> People talk about all the things you can find on museum websites: interactive tours, documents to read, precious objects to look at. None of these are accessible to someone who cannot see the screen. It is not as if the technology does not exist. What would happen if there was a button to click on to get a description of an image, in the same way that you can enlarge an image? . . . Think of the creative capital that could be made out of producing audio descriptions of visuals. (Lisney et al. 2013, 358)

When ideas such as these are not integrated directly into the structure of an exhibit or activity, it can be harder for patrons to take advantage of your services. While not all patrons will be served by each particular innovation, providing avenues to access will help create a more inclusive environment at your library and will help you work to connect with and engage a wider number of patrons.

Accessibility can take many forms, from ensuring that there are routes with elevator access for scavenger hunts to providing paper copies of the clues in a library mystery game in case patrons do not have the relevant technology. It can include using software to ensure that websites are navigable by people with visual impairments and providing sign-language interpreters. It is important to keep in mind that accessibility is about helping your patrons get access to the programs you provide—it is not an optional extra. Your user population will help you determine what types of modifications you may need to make to your activities. Ignoring access issues can alienate and frustrate patrons, which is an especially sad outcome in the context of games. It is important to make sure that your games are playable by all the people in your library.

Basic Accessibility Guidelines

A framework for learning accessibility from the National Center on Universal Design for Learning focuses on three "primary principles":

1. Provide multiple means of representation.
2. Provide multiple means of action and expression.
3. Provide multiple means of engagement. (2014)

Suggestions for implementing these three principles in education are included on the National Center on Universal Design for Learning website (www.udlcenter.org/aboutudl/udlguidelines), but it may be helpful to outline the meaning behind the primary principles here. "Multiple means of representation" means that information should be accessible by the student—for instance, in the right language, adjustable by volume and text size, etc., and accessible in terms of student understanding. "Multiple means of action and expression" encourages students to respond to materials and information in their own way—for example, out loud or using a computer. The use of a variety of different media is essential here. Lastly, "multiple means of engagement" means that material should engage students, give them choices and autonomy, and keep them inspired to keep working (National Center on Universal Design for Learning 2014).

The Association of Specialized and Cooperative Library Agencies (ASCLA), a division of the American Library Association (ALA), provides guidelines and information about providing library services to people who have disabilities (www.ala.org/ascla/asclaissues/libraryservices). Although these guidelines are not specific to game design, they may be a useful place to start.

Looking more specifically at game design, on the site Game Accessibility Guidelines (http://gameaccessibilityguidelines.com/), various contributors, including designers, researchers, and academics, provide general ground rules about designing video games with access in mind. The site sorts its list of considerations and suggestions into basic, intermediate, and advanced categories based on the interplay between three criteria:

- Reach (the number of people who benefit)
- Impact (the difference made to those people)
- Value (the cost to implement)

This site pays particular attention to considering the following types of disabilities: general access, motor control, cognitive, visual, hearing, and speech. Though the site's focus is on the creation of video games, its principles may be easily applied to other types of games as well. Additionally, the framework of areas to consider may be a helpful checklist as you attempt to see your game from different angles. Some suggestions may be good commonsense rules of thumb for all players, such as "Use simple clear language," "Ensure controls are as simple as possible," "Use an easily readable default font size," and "Include an option to adjust the game speed" (Game Accessibility Guidelines 2016).

ASCLA tipsheets for providing services to patrons with various types of disabilities offer more specific guidelines—however, there are many general suggestions that apply to all patrons. These include

- Speak directly to patrons without treating assistants or caregivers as go-betweens.
- Involve patrons in activities.
- Communicate clearly and concisely, and speak naturally.
- Avoid assumptions, and treat all patrons with respect. (2010)

While these are general guidelines that do not necessarily have to do with games, keeping them in mind as you plan will allow you to design an experience for patrons that is as sensitive to individual needs as possible.

⊚ Accessibility Examples and Suggestions

Your patrons, your library context, and your goals for the activity will have a large impact on the design of your game. Games designed for use by the general public should take into consideration the needs of your audience, with an eye toward the needs of people who may have physical or learning disabilities or who may not have access to technology. There are many types of disabilities, and it is not always possible to tell whether a person has a disability. Ideally, patrons with disabilities should not need to inform you of their disability. For this reason, as you plan your game, you should think about ways it can be played by as many people as possible.

It is preferable to make participation in your game seamless, without requiring patrons to disclose health information, but it is also important to provide accommodations if need be. If you are planning a game for a more structured class, you most likely have information about the patrons you are hoping to reach, and this can help you tailor your activity toward their needs—a good teaching strategy in general. Many published suggestions for making games and other activities more inclusive focus on tailoring your activity to the needs of one specific group of people. You will probably need to think beyond one group as you move forward in the planning process, but these suggestions can help you kick start your planning process and help you work to ensure that your game will include as many people as possible. Below are some ways that games and activities might be modified to better meet your patrons' needs.

Jeopardy! Game Modifications

In "Modifying 'Jeopardy!' Games to Benefit All Students," Kathleen Rotter suggests making adaptations to the Jeopardy! format in order to better include students who may have mild learning disabilities. She suggests that teachers

- Encourage notetaking
- Provide organizational strategies to help student recall—guides, memory aids, etc.
- Allow students to work in groups or pairs, and to play the game multiple times (2004)

Allowing students to take and use notes gives them a chance to think about the topics that will be covered by the game ahead of time and to organize their thoughts. Rotter identifies the need for more time with assignments and difficulty remembering facts and information as potential problems students may experience when playing this type of game, and these suggestions are meant to help alleviate these possible difficulties.

Closed Captioning for Screencasts

Many libraries have produced short screencasts designed to help patrons understand concepts, use library tools, and learn new material. Generally, these are brief and focus on one particular skill or group of skills—for example, searching in a database, locating e-books, or using a patron library account. While screencasts can be a great way to provide quick information to patrons, both in and outside the context of a game, remember that you will need to provide captions to go along with your production. Meredith Farkas (2014) suggests writing a script before you create your screencast, which will make it easier for you to provide captions later on. This will help you ensure that your work is accessible to a higher number of people.

Considering Your Audience for a Scavenger Hunt–Style Game

Librarians at the State Library of Queensland in Brisbane, Australia, developed a mobile scavenger hunt–style game in order to better connect with patrons between the ages of eight and fourteen. Incorporating QR codes, a leaderboard, and augmented reality to move players through library spaces, the game focused on providing a primer on library spaces and services (Fitz-Walter et al. 2012). The game was played on iOS smartphones, and patrons who did not have their own device to use could check out a device from the library. While the librarians concluded that mobile devices can be a good hosting platform for various games, they also discovered some challenges. One parent suggested that the library provide a "cheat sheet" that would help parents orient their children to game practices, and others were interested in the possibility of using the game on Android phones.

This game's audience had a profound influence on the game's reception. Because the patrons were mainly children, gearing parts of the game toward their caregivers could help things run smoothly. Usability testing was instrumental in both evaluating the game and improving it for future use.

Access to Technology

Technology access is important to the success of many games and may be a consideration for you as you plan. According to the Pew Research Center, 84 percent of American adults were Internet users in 2015, a number that had grown steadily since 2000 (2015). Many library games and activities center on the use of the Internet, particularly through smartphones, and it is easy to see why: smartphones can provide virtual tours, ask quiz questions, and offer conduits for doing research. That being said, smartphones and the Internet are not fail-safe. Wi-fi goes down. Sites crash. And not every patron has access to a cell phone or mobile device they can use in the course of a tour.

How can you ensure that your game stays accessible to patrons even if they have no access to the Internet or a smartphone? One way to help is to provide options. Many tours and scavenger hunt–type activities can be reconfigured with paper. Questions and directions can be the same or similar, and patrons can choose to complete the activity via the Internet or paper. In some cases, patrons may prefer to use paper even if they have access to the online version. Depending on your funding situation, it also may be possible to provide devices that can be checked out to patrons who wish to complete the activity. While there are some security and other considerations at play here, you may be able to provide devices that can be used just to play your game. Directions that detail how to access online resources can be included as well, and patrons may be able to experiment with library websites from public computers.

Although gaps between people who have access to various kinds of technology appear to be decreasing, it is important not to alienate patrons who may not be able (or may not be willing) to complete your activity using mobile devices. Providing options can go a long way toward establishing trust with patrons and ensuring that they are able to connect with resources available at the library.

ⓖ Questions to Ask

As you refine your game to make sure it provides all patrons with access, you may want to use the following questions as a jumping-off point. These questions do not address every potential accommodation and certainly make no claim to being comprehensive; however, they may be helpful as you consider ways to make sure your game will reach as many of your patrons as possible. Keep in mind as well that your game should be fun—accommodations are simply a way to make sure that more people can be involved.

- Can patrons with limited mobility play your game? For example, is there elevator access to upper floors?
- Are there ways to play the game without the use of technological devices? For example, is it possible to provide a paper version of your online game? Will you keep devices in the library for patrons to check out if they want to play the game? If patrons will be checking out devices to complete the game, are there enough available?
- If your game involves PowerPoint slides, Microsoft Word, or other common tools, are you taking advantage of built-in accessibility features, such as headings in Word that make text easier to navigate or hypertext that saves readers with visual impairments from having to listen to the computer read out entire URLs?
- If your game involves video, can you provide a transcript or closed-captioning so that people with hearing impairments don't miss any of the content?
- Does your game include colors or patterns that may be difficult for people with color blindness to process?
- Is there a way to describe particular visuals from the game so that people with vision impairments understand their connotations?
- What assumptions does your game make about patrons' familiarity with technology? Will you need to provide additional information describing how to do the things patrons will need to do?
- Can patrons work together in pairs or teams to play your game? Conversely, is it possible for individuals to work on their own if they would like to?
- How will you communicate your game's goals to your patrons?

ⓖ Making the Library Stars Tour Accessible

Several accessibility features are already embedded in the Library Stars Tour, but it may be worth noting where they are and how they can help provide better access. Additionally, there are other ways the tour could be made even more accessible. As a project that reflects the needs and circumstances of library patrons, the tour should constantly evolve in order to stay relevant.

The tour is self-paced, and patrons can choose when and with whom (if anyone) to complete it, which affords them a good deal of built-in autonomy. There is no pressure to finish the tour in a set time frame either, though it may be helpful for library staff and writing faculty to emphasize this noncompetitive aspect to students before the tour starts. Though competition can be fun in some contexts, it is not the point of this game, and student sabotage of game materials (moving books around, etc.) in the name of competition can cause problems. Some ways the tour is accessible include

- Player choice of format. Players can decide whether to use a paper version, a version on a device they can check out, or a version that can be accessed on their own device. These versions provide the same materials in different formats—for example, the photos are easily accessible in digitized or physical format, and both include detailed captions that describe what patrons are seeing to ensure that they are accessible to people with visual impairments. The paper and online versions contain the same materials, and both serve a purpose: the paper version means that students do not need to depend on a device, and the online or digital version has more built-in resources that can help students with some disabilities.
- Although the tour requires that patrons physically traverse the library, there are elevators available in addition to stairs. Library maps (included in the tour package) indicate elevator locations, in addition to staircase locations.
- Choice about whether to complete the tour in small groups or as individuals allows players to determine for themselves how they will feel the most comfortable.

Although many patrons may find these accessibility measures sufficient to allow them to complete the tour, others may need additional accommodations, which should also be made available. These accommodations include

- Materials in Braille, including descriptions of images
- Availability of screen-reader tools, such as JAWS (www.freedomscientific.com/Products/Blindness/JAWS)
- Ensuring tour routes always allow enough room both for people who are walking and people who are using wheelchairs to navigate the space

One benefit of the tour's tight connection with introductory writing classes is that writing instructors are likely to be at least somewhat familiar with additional accommodations that may be needed for tour participants, and they can serve as a resource to library staff planners. Good relationships with writing faculty and the ability to work with them to best help students is helpful in this regard.

Of course, not all library projects will be collaborations between librarians and faculty—some will involve community members, families, and other stakeholders.

Even a relatively simple game like this one will require detailed thought about how it can be made more inclusive. Careful evaluation of feedback and an open mind about refining the game will be essential. If patrons do approach to discuss other accommodations, it is important to take their concerns seriously and to work with them to find a way that they can participate.

◎ Key Points

This chapter discussed ways you can make your game available to all patrons. Game accommodations should not be considered nice-to-have extras—it is important to think about ways your game can reach as many people as possible. Many types of accommodations will depend on the needs of individual patrons and should keep them closely in mind.

- Games can be beneficial to all patrons.
- There are many guidelines that will help you work to provide accessible games.

- Accessible games will benefit a large number of patrons rather than just a few.
- Sensitivity to individual needs is important—be respectful of patrons and work to provide accessible services for them.
- Don't assume that all patrons have access to technology or that they understand how to use it. Although many patrons will be familiar with mobile devices and other tools, some will not be.
- The Library Stars Tour enhances its accessibility by providing information in different formats, including Braille and materials that are readable by screen reader software; ensuring that patrons have enough space to maneuver through the library; and giving patrons choice where possible.

In the next chapter, you will learn how you can assess your game in order to learn what is working well and figure out how it can be changed to be even more effective.

References

Americans with Disabilities Act of 1990, as Amended. 2009. www.ada.gov/pubs/adastatute08.pdf.

Association of Specialized and Cooperative Library Agencies (ASCLA). 2010. "Library Accessibility—What You Need to Know." www.ala.org/ascla/asclaprotools/accessibilitytipsheets.

Barlet, Mark C., and Steve D. Spohn. 2013. *Includification: A Practical Guide to Game Accessibility.* www.includification.com/AbleGamers_Includification.pdf.

Farkas, Meredith. 2014. "More than Words." *American Libraries* 45, no. 5 (May): 20–20.

Fitz-Walter, Zachary, Dian Tjondronegoro, Desmond Koh, and Michael Zrobok. 2012. "Mystery at the Library: Encouraging Library Exploration Using a Pervasive Mobile Game." Proceedings of the 24th Australian Computer-Human Interaction Conference, 142–45.

Game Accessibility Guidelines. 2016. "A Straightforward Reference for Inclusive Game Design." http://gameaccessibilityguidelines.com/.

Lisney, Eleanor, Jonathan Bowen, Kirsten Hearn, and Maria Zedda. 2013. "Museums and Technology: Being Inclusive Helps Accessibility for All." *Curator* 56, no. 3 (July): 353–61.

National Center on Universal Design for Learning. 2014. "UDL Guidelines—Version 2.0." www.udlcenter.org/aboutudl/udlguidelines.

Pew Research Center. 2015. "Americans' Internet Access: 2000–2015." www.pewinternet.org/2015/06/26/americans-internet-access-2000-2015/.

Pryal, Katie Rose Guest. 2016. "This Is What Accessibility Looks Like (Part 2)." http://katieroseguestpryal.com/2016/04/05/this-is-what-accessibility-looks-like-part-2/.

Rotter, Kathleen. 2004. "Modifying 'Jeopardy!' Games to Benefit All Students." *Teaching Exceptional Children* 36 (3): 58.

Wray, Christina C. 2013. "Practical Strategies for Making Online Library Services and Instruction Accessible to All Patrons." *Journal of Library & Information Services in Distance Learning* 7 (4): 360–71.

Game Assessment

HOW DO YOU KNOW WHEN you did something well? Runners often strive for PRs, or personal records: their individual best time in an event or at a particular distance. Baseball pitchers might measure themselves in ERAs, or earned run averages. Similarly, students in a class might measure progress using pre- and post-test results, or by looking at their grades in a particular class in one semester. Each of these assessment measures attempts to evaluate progress and accomplishment. Without some sort of framework to point to, quantifying an experience can get foggy—maybe you feel like you learned a lot in a class, but it's hard to put into words exactly what you learned; or maybe you remember a class fondly, but you can't quite remember why. Assessment, which can take the form of surveys, informal conversations, quizzes, or portfolios, among other options, can give you a clearer sense of which things worked and what there is left to improve on. Overall, they can help you take strides toward ascertaining how well you did in both the classroom and other settings where there is a goal to be accomplished.

The examples above vary widely—you could not use an ERA, for example, to determine how well a student did in a history class—and this is important. Assessment should closely reflect the skills being examined, and it should have a clear goal. Frequent formal and informal game assessment, tailored toward your goals for the game and the objectives you are trying to achieve, will help you determine whether or not your game is successful. It will also help you decide how you can best adapt your game to meet the needs of your users. Assessment can be conducted at almost any stage of the game process, from initial brainstorming sessions onward, and there is no need to limit yourself to one form of assessment. While assessment can be comprehensive and multifaceted, it can also be relatively simple, involving strategies such as student surveys or scanning the results of small quizzes. No matter how big or small your game is, assessment will be a key aspect of its success and its evolution over time.

Like many other facets of the game experience, assessment is intrinsically linked to the goals that you have for your activity. Your goals will help you frame the questions you want to ask about your game and will give you a good sense of whether or not your game was a success. There are several ways this may work. For example, if one of your goals is that students will be able to find books in a school library using the Dewey Decimal system, a measure of assessment may be the number of questions students ask about book location before and after completing the game. Will all of these questions be tied to activities that taught students about the Dewey Decimal system? Most likely not—there may easily be students who missed your activity, or there may be questions from students who attended and didn't understand everything—still, taken in conjunction with other measures, this information can help you get a handle on the success of the game and what students learned. You also may try developing a quiz that students can take, or a relay race where they need to correctly shelve or organize books before moving on to the next step. While assessment can take many forms, it should help you answer a direct question—or several—that you have about your game's effectiveness.

Establishing clear goals from the start will help with this process. Compare the following two goals.

1. Students will understand the Dewey Decimal system.
2. Students will be able to locate books shelved using the Dewey Decimal system.

The first goal is conceptual and may be hard to firmly grasp. How can you ever really know, after all, how well another human being understands something? The vagueness of the goal will make it harder to assess, though you may try to get a sense of it via quizzes, essays, or detailed student explanations. The second goal, however, is relatively easy to test: you can ask students to locate books and see if they can do it. There may be more nuance required here—for example, you may want students to locate books within a particular time span or to be able to take them to the appropriate shelf—but for the most part the stated goal spells out exactly how you can assess it to determine student success.

In *Understanding by Design*, Grant Wiggins and Jay McTighe describe what they call "a continuum of assessments" that can be used by teachers to find out whether or not they have met their goals for an assignment (2005, 152). This continuum includes

- Informal checks for understanding
- Observations and dialogues
- Tests and quizzes
- Academic prompts
- Performance tasks

By using a variety of these methods, Wiggins and McTighe note, it is possible to get a more rounded picture of how well students understand what they have learned. While game-inspired activities played in a library are not exactly the same as projects encountered by a class in school, some combination of these sorts of assessment measures will give you a more detailed picture of your project's success than you can get from just one. In the Dewey Decimal system example earlier, students' work may culminate in correctly shelving books (a performance task), but it may also include discussions with individual students, tests, or quizzes on how to read the catalog, and other measures. A rubric for understanding an individual student's learning might look like the example in figure 9.1.

Some topics are harder to assess than others. For example, if your goal is to figure out whether your game encouraged students to ask questions when they needed help, it may be difficult to determine their exact motivations and whether your game contributed. Surveys and interviews paired with completed tasks and more informal conversations can help you try to get to the bottom of some of these questions, and assessment at various game stages may help you get a better feel for why your students or patrons act in the ways they do.

Authentic Assessment and Traditional Assessment

Assessment can take various forms but has a tendency to veer in one of two directions. These are authentic assessment and traditional assessment approaches. Traditional assessment means quizzes, tests, standardized tests, reports, and other methods. You may end up using some of these assessment methods to evaluate your game. In more recent years, however, teachers have begun to emphasize authentic assessment techniques, which require students to more explicitly prove that they have gained the skills they need via real-life demonstration. Think of third graders solving division problems on a quiz as traditional assessment, and then think of those same third graders dividing a freshly baked pizza into even slices as an authentic assessment. In *Becoming a Better Teacher: Eight Innovations That Work*, Giselle O. Martin-Kniep identifies the following "attributes of authenticity" that can be used to evaluate whether a task used for assessment can be labeled authentic.

- Real purpose and audience
- Integration of content and skills
- Disciplined inquiry/academic rigor
- Explicit standards and scoring criteria
- Elaborate communication
- Levels of thinking
- Reflection, self- and peer-assessment, and feedback
- Flexibility in content, strategies, products, and time (2000, 28)

For example, middle school students in a K–8 school might play a game that teaches them about using the Dewey Decimal system to find books and materials. After the

Dewey Decimal Project Student Name:_____	
Criteria	**Student Score**
Pre-quiz	
Participated in library game (y/n)	
Number of books shelved correctly (out of 10)	
Post-quiz	
Reflection completed (y/n)	

Figure 9.1. Rubric for understanding an individual student's learning

game, they might accompany students in lower grades on their library visits and re-shelve the books the children are finished with. Librarians can then check the stacks when they are finished to make sure that they have put everything back in the right order. This solves a real-world problem (re-shelving books between classes) and allows the middle school students to demonstrate that they understand what they have learned. Discussions after the session could help further cement student understanding of the Dewey Decimal system, as could other measurement methods.

Portfolios of collected work may also be used as authentic assessment measures. For example, at school and academic libraries, librarians and teachers or faculty may work together to develop games that instruct students over the course of the semester and then may look at sections of student portfolios to see more organically whether these games had an impact. For example, bibliographies in student research papers can be consulted and evaluated to see if students used appropriate sources. End-of-semester compilations of student work, alongside written reflections about what students have learned, can be curated to help determine the success of library activities. Reflections are key to portfolios—students should be able to discuss what they have learned and not simply provide a collection of materials they have produced. The materials included should show some sign of thought as well, rather than simply showcasing the student's ability to put papers into a folder or file. Jon Mueller includes suggestions and guidelines for using portfolios to evaluate student progress on his website Authentic Assessment Toolbox (http://jfmueller.faculty.noctrl.edu/toolbox/portfolios.htm).

Asking Questions

Before you decide how to structure your assessment, you will want to think carefully about what, exactly, you are trying to learn from it. The following questions may help you get started and may prompt you to think of other questions that address issues more specifically linked to your game.

- What was the purpose of the game?
- What goals did you identify?
- What did you want patrons to be able to do after they had finished?
- What are some ways you can tell that your goals have been accomplished?
- What is an appropriate measure of the goals you are assessing?
- Were the goals of the library met?
- Were the goals of stakeholders met?
- What should participants have taken away from their involvement with the game and how do you know they have?
- Do the results of the assessment suggest changes you may make in the future?
- Do the results of the assessment suggest other questions or activities that you might want to ask or consider?

Types of Assessments

As with so many other aspects of the gamification experience, your assessment's form and structure will be closely influenced by the structure of your activity and by what you are trying to learn about it. That being said, assessments for library activities and events have taken the following forms, among others: quizzes and tests; informal interviews; portfolio or other material evaluations; surveys; task completion; and participation. Some of these are addressed below.

Quizzes and Tests

If your game is designed to teach its players about library services and resources, quizzes and tests can frequently help you determine what players have learned. Short quizzes can tell you, for example, if students know how to connect to a library VPN or proxy, or if they know how to find the library's maps on the website. While quizzes and tests are not perfect—there is no guarantee, for example, that students will retain in the long term the information they have acquired—they can at least give you a snapshot of what players took away as they worked their way through.

Quizzes and tests can also be used as a way to check in with students. A small quiz for understanding after the completion of a game may help determine whether and what patrons learned from the experience. While quizzes and tests will not tell you everything about a participant's understanding, they can help you get a quick read on what information is sticking, and this can inform future versions of your game.

Informal Interviews

In some library settings, it may be possible to arrange quick interviews with patrons as they complete your activity. You might strike up a conversation about whether players enjoyed the activity, or whether they feel it met their needs. Though these types of assessments can be difficult to quantify, they nevertheless can provide feedback that may be helpful as you continue to work with your game. One benefit to these types of conversations is their informality—patrons may be more likely to share honest feedback with you outside a more focused assessment context. Informal interviews can also help you become more connected to your patrons and allow you the chance to get to know them better.

Portfolios/Evaluations of Materials

Portfolios, discussed briefly earlier, can be helpful as well. In a school library, for example, participation in library activities may be designed to help students conduct library research and find books on different topics. Collaboration with classroom teachers may allow librarians to look at student papers to get a sense of the results of student participation in library activities. Portfolios can highlight what the student thought was important (for example, they probably won't mention the library if they didn't find it to be useful), and they can also showcase whether or not students are using the skills you had hoped they would in their assignments. Arguably, portfolios are a way to evaluate student learning more holistically, which in turn gives you a clearer picture of what they understand. Because portfolios help to give a snapshot of how much a student understands overall, they may be a good source of information when evaluating games that are tied to curriculum.

Surveys

Though similar to quizzes, surveys are designed to gather information without providing a grade or other feedback. Surveys can focus on how well the activity met participant needs, with questions such as "Did you find this activity to be helpful?" "What can we do in the future to improve player experience?" and "Did you run into any difficulties?" In situations where it might be hard to begin a casual conversation with patrons as they finish, surveys can give you candid feedback about how things went. The feedback you get will be most helpful if it is anonymous so that participants don't feel like they will offend you.

Task Completion Activities

For some games, determining who was able to finish may be a form of assessment. If your game requires that students find a book or database, for example, or use clues provided by the game to answer a question, it may be that the game itself is testing them and that completion rates can show in part how successful students were in accomplishing the game's objectives. If your game is structured so that students need to complete it in order to accomplish its goals, you will guarantee that all finishers have at least figured out how to win the game. If the game is voluntary, however, requiring players to finish may make them want to drop out. It is also possible that cheating rates will rise, especially if participants are required to finish the game for a class and can't figure out how to do so.

In other contexts, however, task completion assessments can be incorporated into the activity. Especially in school and academic libraries, partnerships with teachers and professors may allow you to finish your game with an activity that shows whether or not and what students learned. As with so many other things game-related, a lot will ride on your context.

Participation Rates and Gate Counts

Depending on the goal of your activity, the number of participants may be a measure you can use for assessment. For example, if you plan to stage an after-hours tag game in order to reach out to your local community, it is easy to make a case that the number of participants (or the number of returning participants for a weekly or monthly event) will help to gauge whether or not the game was or is a success. Since games should, if possible, be completed at the discretion of their players, whether or not people want to participate can give you a good feel for your level of success. Similarly, if the goal of your game is to encourage more patrons to visit the library, comparing gate counts before and after the launch of the game may be a good form of assessment.

⊚ Assessing the Library Stars Tour Game

The Library Stars Tour, like many games and projects used in library outreach to patrons, can be assessed in many ways. Its context as a result of a partnership between the library and faculty in introductory writing classes means that many forms of assessment, such as surveys, portfolio analysis, and quizzes, that may not be available in other cases are available here. It is possible to assess the game by asking students to complete a short survey as they finish, and this could include open-ended questions such as

- What is your biggest take-away from this activity?
- Do you feel more comfortable using the library as a result of completing this tour?
- Do you have any comments or suggestions?

The open-ended nature of the questions allows participants the opportunity to provide more candid responses—since there is no right answer, librarians can get a better feel for how the game came across. Also, since students are not being tested on what they learned, a survey can contribute to a more comfortable environment. There could also be more informational quiz questions designed to determine whether patrons learned as a result of their participation, such as

- Can you name a database you plan to use for your research?
- Where would you find a book with call number _____?
- What are three different ways you can get help in the library?

Either the quiz option, the survey option, or a combination of both could be useful in determining what students will take from their time spent with the activity and whether or not they learned what librarians were hoping they would.

That being said, the Library Stars Tour also focuses heavily on trying to make students feel more comfortable using library spaces, and it's hard to get at whether that was successful through a survey or quiz. In this case, rather than relying solely on results gathered at the end of the activity, it may be of more interest for librarians to look at records: Are more students coming to the library to study? Has there been an increase in the number of reference questions that have to do with assignments traditionally completed by first-year students? How many people turned in raffle tickets for the prize at the end?

Interviews with students may be of interest here as well. Librarians might invite student participants to share their thoughts over pizza, for example, or might conduct small focus groups to discuss what worked well and what didn't. Questions in these kinds of scenarios might include

- What did you think of the Library Stars Tour? Was it helpful?
- What did you learn from it?
- Would you recommend it to new students? Why or why not?
- Do you have any comments or suggestions about ways the library can make the Library Stars Tour better?

It also may be possible to network with participating faculty members or other collaborators to see if they can share overheard comments or portfolio assessment measures. Faculty may expressly ask students whether they enjoyed the activity, or they might compile information they gained through student journals or comments to share anonymously with librarians. This more casual communication may be a source of particularly insightful feedback since students are sharing what they really feel rather than what they think the library might expect.

Employing a number of assessment methods is in keeping with Wiggins and Mc-Tighe's admonishment to consider a pattern of results (2005). If participating students perform poorly on the quiz part of the assessment but all other indicators show that they are using the library more, conducting more thorough research, and asking questions more frequently at the reference desk, it does not make sense to conclude that the tour has no value at all. There may be ways that tour questions and instructions can be rephrased, or there may be other issues at play that are having an effect on student performance.

Assessment can be hard. Like many other games and activities, both inside and outside libraries, the Library Stars Tour may be difficult to fully assess. Considering its results from different angles may provide feedback that helps to ensure the tour is doing what it is supposed to. While it is important to assess activities planned for students, there is also a balance to be kept between making sure that an activity is useful and appropriate and staying true to the activity's aims. At a certain point too, most activities will come to the end of their lifecycle and need to be retired to make room for fresher, more relevant material.

Key Points

This chapter discussed ways to think about, plan, and conduct assessments that will tell you about the success of your game. Assessment can help you determine how well your game accomplished its goals and can give you a sense of what areas may be ripe for revision. Multiple assessments in different forms will give you more information about the overall success of the activity. Measurable goals, set ahead of time, will help you assess the most important parts of your activity.

- Assessment measures should be tied to your goals.
- Assessment measures should reflect your game's purpose and structure.
- Assessment measures can help you make revisions to your game.
- Assessment measures can take many forms, including quizzes and tests; informal interviews; portfolios or other material evaluation; surveys; task completion; and participation in class activities.
- It is better to use multiple measures of assessment—for example, small, informal quizzes and then a culminating task that asks patrons to demonstrate what they have learned.

Assessment is an important tool in the life and evolution of your project and will help it grow and develop along with your patrons and library. The next chapter will provide a summary of the major points of this book.

References

Martin-Kniep, Giselle O. 2000. *Becoming a Better Teacher: Eight Innovations That Work*. Alexandria, VA: Association for Supervision and Curriculum Development.
Wiggins, Grant P., and Jay McTighe. 2005. *Understanding by Design*. Alexandria, VA: Association for Supervision and Curriculum Development.

Themes and Predictions

ON JULY 6, 2016, Pokémon Go launched in the United States. Almost immediately the Internet was awash with reports of people wandering around staring at their smartphones; reports of Pokémon Go–related crimes; and social media photos of Pokémon creatures in the real world. Pokémon Go (www.pokemongo.com/en-us/) is an augmented reality game that uses smartphone mapping software to add images of game characters to users' phone screens as they explore their actual world, letting them play the game at home, at work, or in parks, airports, businesses, and open spaces, for example. Wherever players might be in the real world, they can find and capture these creatures. Captured Pokémon can then be used in gameplay. Pokémon Go was hugely popular from practically the moment it launched and sparked a nationwide discussion about the game and its implications. Because Pokémon Go shifted video gameplay into the physical world, it blurred the (already increasingly blurry) lines between games and life and suggested the potential for other types of augmented reality games. Additionally, and perhaps more importantly, Pokémon Go's success highlighted games' capacity to grab their players' attention and have a lasting impact both inside and outside the game.

Games and Real Life

People frequently use game metaphors to talk about their lives. Working situations to individual advantage is "gaming the system"; the end of an arduous project becomes "the finish line"; shifting expectations is "moving the goalposts"; and "batting 1000" is performing particularly well at a given task. Games can often be apt comparisons to real life—they involve having an objective, working toward it, and ultimately they end in either success or failure. Using them as descriptions can thread an implied storyline into our lives—we were here and these things happened for a reason; life is not just meaningless and random.

Additionally, games can help us understand our relationships with other people. MTV has a long-running series called *The Challenge* (www.mtv.com/shows/the-challenge-rivals-iii) that pits former MTV reality show stars against each other in teams to win money. Though the participants often have long and complicated (and extensively documented) personal histories and dramas, one of the central draws of the show is watching them come together to work cooperatively to accomplish their goals. Even the most contentious feud may be dampened or nuanced by the contestants' need to trust and rely on one another as they climb mountains, balance on narrow beams, and attempt to solve puzzles. In fact, this is often a major plot point of the show.

In short, games do not seem out of place in the context of real life—they provide texture and structure, and they help us understand goals and achievement. Games can bring people together and encourage them to work constructively. This is a powerful pull. While not everything in a library context (or, really, anywhere) can or should be presented in game format, adding games and game elements to particular tasks and areas—such as instruction sessions, circulation processes, and library spaces—can encourage patrons to move beyond their initial comfort zones and reach out to new people. Games can insert energy into what may otherwise seem like boring or mundane tasks, and they can help people engage more effectively with what they are doing. Games can give us new ways to see the world.

◎ Games in Libraries: A Summary

Games can be used in libraries in many ways and for many purposes. In particular, this book explored the following aspects and ramifications of using games.

- Personalizing games to engage users and bring them into the action
- Setting game goals and aligning them with what players want
- Designing games for use in library settings in order to appeal to various audiences, preferences, and needs
- Identifying and collaborating with potential game partners who can both enrich and expand the relevance of your game
- Considering what types of games might be most feasible in particular environments and settings
- Incorporating games and game aspects into instruction
- Ensuring that games are accessible and available to all library patrons
- Assessing games in order to evaluate their success and build upon them in the future

Because new games are being created every day, it is impossible to fully explore every challenge or benefit that might arise from their use. Overall, however, there are several themes braided through the discussion of how to create and maintain games that will fit within library services.

1. **Your game should reflect the needs, context, and goals of your particular audience**. In the Library Stars Tour, the game's structure as a social scavenger-hunt assigned

by writing instructors was heavily influenced by its place in the curriculum and the fact that its players were new college students who were relatively unfamiliar with the library, the city, and each other. The game sought to make its players comfortable while at the same time introducing them to new places and resources. It was possible for the game to be fairly intensive because students needed to complete it as a part of their coursework. At the same time, the game kept a light-hearted feel in order to reduce library anxiety and encourage players to ask for help. A game in a different context—for example, an elementary school library that hosts a theme night related to a common read—might look totally different.

While library goals are important to the design of a successful game, keeping player goals in mind is even more so. Players won't want to spend time doing something that they get nothing out of—in order to appeal to them, games need to help them do or get something that they want. A game that players enjoy and that helps them meet their goals will also be more successful at helping the library accomplish its own goals.

2. **The planning and implementation of your game is a team effort and will most likely require the help of collaborators and helpers, both inside and outside the library**. Just as movie credits acknowledge the efforts and expertise of a dazzlingly large number of people, your game's success will depend on the work of a committed team of partners and experts. These partners may come from the library—they may be leads in other areas, for instance, or volunteers, or student assistants. They may also come from outside the library, in the form of community stakeholders, local businesses, or other university departments. Aligning your game with their goals will give your game credibility and allow it to reach a wider audience.

The Library Stars Tour, for example, drew on academic partners—writing instructors whose students needed to use library resources in order to be successful—in addition to community members such as owners of local businesses who provided prizes and helped with events. Library staff who wanted to connect with students were also involved and helped to put a face to library services. These collaborations provided a way to see the game from outside a library perspective and helped to embed the game in the culture of the library's community. Despite their importance, libraries can be at times overlooked—working with stakeholders and partners can help your library instead shine a spotlight on how it can help patrons.

3. **You should be constantly aware of the context and setting of your game and of how it fits into the larger community of the library**. Libraries are, necessarily, specialized. Corporate libraries, for example, will face different challenges and opportunities than will high school libraries or law libraries. Because of this, you will want to think carefully about who your patrons are and what their needs might be. In designing games that appeal to them, you will need to consider your patrons' lives and circumstances in addition to thinking about your library's situation, goals, and needs. Game programming for senior citizens at a public library may have a different focus than programming for incoming law students.

You will also want to think of ways to ensure that your game is as accessible as possible to the widest number of patrons. Provide paper versions of electronic games, for example, and make sure there are easily used game routes that can be navigated by wheelchair users. Whenever possible or necessary, try to provide game instructions and information in different languages. It may not be possible for every game to be exactly the same for every person, but it is still important to try to make the experience equivalent.

Not everything needs to be a game. Certainly, for most people their morning commute is best framed as a contemplative experience rather than as one that involves point scoring and competition. But there is no denying that games can have a powerful impact on their players and that, with good design, careful planning, and appeal to players, games can be hugely influential, not just in the moment, but in life in general. Thoughtful consideration of where games might fit best, and how they might serve as a complement to other library services, will allow you to design patron experiences that are relevant, rich, and well-suited to your library.

◎ Games in the Future

The Entertainment Software Association (2016) reports that "the average age of the most frequent game purchaser is 38," contradicting the stereotype of video game players as being predominantly teenagers and young men. In addition, games are frequently played and used by parents with their children, 95 percent of whom say they "always or sometimes [pay] attention to video games played by their child." And a whopping 63 percent of surveyed households in the United States include "at least one person who plays video games regularly (3 hours or more per week)." These facts underline the popularity of video games in today's world and help to demonstrate their appeal across ages and genders. Though libraries may or may not include game programming and activities in video game format, it is hard to deny that games by themselves are widely popular. As libraries work to connect with their patrons, game design and use may go up.

Video games are not the only games in town either. Board and card games have seen something of a renaissance, with offerings like Pandemic, Settlers of Catan, Exploding Kittens, Unexploded Cows, and Ticket to Ride proving that there is a market for games that take place off-screen as well. Ashley Gross (2016) reports that board game sales rose 20 percent in 2015—which is not a bad feat considering the popularity and ubiquity of games played on smartphones and other devices. Though board games may be difficult to design for use in libraries, their popularity speaks to an interest in playing games overall.

When it comes to games, it is difficult to predict the future. Gamification, in particular, has seen many vocal critics who deride its affiliation with game elements and see it as manipulative and wrong. Ian Bogost, in "Why Gamification Is Bullshit," argues that the application of game aspects to non-game scenarios—especially in business contexts—effectively is a way of applying a rote solution to perceived problems. He writes,

> Overall, gamification's relationship to games isn't just one of exploitation, but also one of total and complete indifference and unconcern. For gamification, games are not a medium capable of producing sophisticated experiences in the service of diverse functions and goals, but merely a convenient rhetorical hook into a state of anxiety in contemporary business. (2014, 76)

Bogost's argument underscores the importance of employing games and game elements where they are appropriate in terms of helping patrons understand library systems and practices rather than just applying them willy-nilly as a sort of cure-all. Games should not be manipulative or used as a means to gain control over patrons. Games deployed carefully can provide helpful complements to existing practices and services, but embedding them everywhere sets patrons up for game burnout and devalues games as potential tools. Don't forget, your game should focus on how best to help and enrich the lives of your patrons rather than serve as a cheap trick to beef up library statistics.

In her book *Reality Is Broken: Why Games Make Us Better and How They Can Change the World*, Jane McGonigal argues that many game metaphors reveal a bias against games: "We don't like to feel that someone is using strategy against us, or manipulating us for their personal amusement" (2011, 19–20). Though McGonigal sees (and praises) many ways that games can have a positive impact on their players and the world, this perceived bias may serve as a caution to librarians working to design games for their patrons. Though games can be influential and valuable, they can also be seen as manipulative, and they should be deployed strategically—as a way to increase engagement during instruction sessions, for example, or as a way to help patrons complete their research and accomplish their personal goals.

In 2012, the Pew Research Center released a report titled "The Future of Gamification." Included in the report were the results of a survey that asked participants to agree or disagree with statements about gamification. The report says,

> Some 53 percent said yes that gamification will be widespread, but a number of them qualified this by saying the evolving adoption of gamification will continue to have some limits. Some 42 percent chose a more modest scenario that predicted gamification will not evolve to be a larger trend except in specific realms. (Anderson and Rainie 2012)

Some years after this study was released, it remains unclear to what extent gamification will continue to grow and evolve within library, business, and other settings. That being said, the natural appeal of games puts them comfortably within the auspices of many library services.

Though it is impossible to know how games will evolve as a part of library services, one benefit to their use is that they are inherently forward-thinking. An unsuccessful game that you run one time gives you the opportunity to learn and adapt as you plan for the future. Just as libraries are constantly moving forward and rethinking old strategies, game design affords us the chance to see things with fresh eyes and to approach—and possibly solve—problems in new and more innovative ways.

Key Points

Games in libraries can serve many different objectives and can provide benefits and connections to a wide number of people both inside and outside the library. Games can engage their players and can help your library community forge new relationships. Above all, games can be a way to bring people together and help them accomplish their goals. Games can be large or small and can work in a variety of contexts—that said, games are not a solution to every problem and should be designed strategically to meet patron and library needs. Done well, games can add spice to existing services and can bring people together in new and valuable ways. Another thing to keep in mind: your game should be fun! That means you should have fun too.

- Games are everywhere, and their popularity highlights how effective they can be.
- People of all ages and backgrounds are interested in games.
- Games can help people make sense of the trajectory of their lives.

- Games should reflect the needs and goals of your specific audience and context.
- Game design offers you the opportunity to work with other partners and learn from their expertise and perspective.
- Games exist in the world, and it is important to be aware of context as you design them.
- Although games are popular, they are not the answer to every question in and of themselves, and they need to be incorporated carefully into their contexts in order to work.
- Adding games to your library services can help you connect with patrons and encourage both patrons and library staff to see the world in new ways.
- Game assessment gives you the chance to constantly rethink and improve your game services and design.

As you plan games in your library, make sure to think carefully and comprehensively about your patrons, context, partners, and needs. But above all, don't forget to make things fun, for both you and your patrons. Happy gaming!

References

Anderson, Janna, and Lee Rainie. 2012. "The Future of Gamification." Pew Research Center. www.pewinternet.org/2012/05/18/the-future-of-gamification/.

Bogost, Ian. 2014. "Why Gamification Is Bullshit." In *The Gameful World*, edited by Steffan P. Walz and Sebastian Deterding, 65–77. Cambridge, MA: MIT Press.

Entertainment Software Association. 2016. *Essential Facts About the Computer and Video Game Industry*. www.theesa.com/wp-content/uploads/2016/04/Essential-Facts-2016.pdf.

Gross, Ashley. 2016. "Amid Board Game Boom, Designers Roll the Dice on Odd Ideas—Even Exploding Cows." NPR. www.npr.org/2016/07/24/484356521/amid-board-game-boom-designers-roll-the-dice-on-odd-ideas-even-exploding-cows.

McGonigal, Jane. 2011. *Reality Is Broken: Why Games Make Us Better and How They Can Change the World*. New York: Penguin Press.

Rosenberg, Gabriel. 2016. "Pokémon Go Is Catching Us All—In Unexpected Ways." NPR. www.npr.org/sections/alltechconsidered/2016/07/11/485551781/pokemon-go-is-catching-us-all-in-unexpected-ways.

Index

About the Author

Elizabeth McMunn-Tetangco holds an MLIS from San Jose State, an MAT from the University of San Francisco, and a BA from the University of California, Berkeley. She works as an instruction librarian at the University of California, Merced. The author of "If You Build It . . . : One Campus' Firsthand Account of Gamification in the Academic Library," published in *College & Research Libraries News*, and coauthor of "Think Like a Researcher: Integrating the Research Process Into the Introductory Composition Curriculum," a chapter in *The New Information Literacy Instruction: Best Practices* (2015), she has long had an interest in using games to connect with students.